Fluency in Focus

Comprehension Strategies for All Young Readers

*Mary Lee Prescott-Griffin
and Nancy L. Witherell*

Heinemann
Portsmouth, NH

KH

Heinemann
A division of Reed Elsevier Inc.
361 Hanover Street
Portsmouth, NH 03801–3912
www.heinemann.com

Offices and agents throughout the world

Library of Congress Cataloging-in-Publication Data
Prescott-Griffin, Mary Lee.
  Fluency in focus : comprehension strategies for all young readers /
Mary Lee Prescott-Griffin and Nancy L. Witherell.
    p. cm.
  Includes bibliographical references.
  ISBN 0-325-00622-9 (alk. paper)
  1. Reading (Elementary)—United States.   2. Reading comprehension.
3. Fluency (Language learning).   I. Witherell, Nancy L.   II. Title.
LB1573.7.P74 2004
372.47—dc22   2004010387

Editor: Kate Montgomery
Production editor: Sonja S. Chapman
Cover and interior design: Jenny Jensen Greenleaf
Compositor: Technologies 'N Typography
Manufacturing: Steve Bernier

Printed in the United States of America on acid-free paper
08   07   06   05   VP   3   4   5

8/26/05

To my sons,
Ransom and Winward,
with love.
—MLPG

With love to the men in my life:
my husband, Peter, and my sons,
Paul, Jonathan, and TC.
—NLW

Contents

Acknowledgments

Beginning with our earliest conversations about fluency and its connections to reading comprehension, our thinking has been nudged and supported by many people.

We thank Mary Lee's colleagues at the Rhode Island Department of Elementary and Secondary Education, most notably Charlotte Diffendale and her "request" for teacher workshops on fluency. Research in preparation for these workshops—part of the Rhode Island Reading Excellence Grant initiative—sent Mary Lee back to the literature to take a fresh look at fluency.

Grateful thanks and sincere admiration go to teachers Sharon Roberts, Kristin Vito, Christine Wiltshire, Sarah Rich, Joy Richardson, and Jenny Baumeister for sharing their expertise and their classrooms. And special thanks to the students and administrators of the L. G. Nourse School, in Norton, Massachusetts; the Fairlawn Early Learning Center, in Lincoln, Rhode Island; the Paul Cuffee Charter School, in Providence, Rhode Island; the Hugh Cole School, in Warren, Rhode Island; and the Mills Pond School, in Smithtown, New York. As always, the students taught us the most—in this case, about what it means to be truly fluent.

We have had the good fortune and great pleasure of working with Kate Montgomery, our editor at Heinemann. We are indebted to her for "redirecting" our proposal, for offering incredibly helpful suggestions, for skillfully editing the manuscript, and for approaching this project with warmth and enthusiasm. Thanks also to Alan Huisman, Sonja Chapman and all at Heinemann who have shepherded our work with care and attention.

Finally, and most especially, we want to thank our families for their support, encouragement, and love.

Introduction

Fluency in Focus: Comprehension Strategies for All Young Readers offers educators the theoretical background as well as the practical tools to help students become fluent, confident readers. To us, disfluency is a little like those annoying cell phone conversations where technical problems, frequent interruptions, and halting repetitions cause us to hang up in exasperation. We do not want children of any age to hang up on reading. Instead, we want them to sing stories and ideas to all who will listen. The tools and strategies outlined here are designed to help them to do just that.

Where does meaning begin for readers? With pictures? With words? With simply picking up a book? Strong readers are continually constructing meaning, accessing prior knowledge, drawing upon literate backgrounds, and attending to semantic, structural, and orthographic cues in order to understand. As readers gain control of letters, sounds, and words, we say they have "broken the code": they are fluent.

The ability to read fluently is one of five component skills of a balanced reading program as recognized by the National Reading Panel (2000), but what do we really mean when we say readers are fluent? Is fluency automatic, accurate reading of text? Or is fluency the very center of meaning? If fluency involves not only speed, accuracy, and automaticity but also the use of appropriate phrasing, intonation, and expression to convey an author's intentions and to demonstrate understanding, then fluency, indeed, lies at the heart of reading comprehension. Fluency, in effect, pulls together all of a developing reader's skills.

When teachers assess children's reading, fluency is often neglected (Allington 1983). When disfluency *is* identified, it is frequently equated with poor word-solving skills, to be remedied by more teaching of letters, sounds, phonics strategies, and vocabulary in isolation.

This book broadens the definition of fluency. It outlines many instructional and assessment strategies that go beyond letter, sound, and word work to build readers' meaning-making skills, thus enabling them to read with deeper fluency than merely saying the words. Besides examining reading rate and accuracy, it also explores phrasing and the use of such elements as pitch, stress, pauses, tone, and expression (Dowhower 1987; Herman 1985).

In the primary grades, fluency (or disfluency) is readily apparent, because children often read aloud. However, as children move into silent reading, fluency (or disfluency) often becomes invisible: disfluent habits such as reading slowly or using halting, choppy phrasing are hidden. Such disfluent behavior severely limits older readers' comprehension of the ideas in the text. As a consequence, when text length and complexity increase, disfluent readers are left behind.

This book provides fluency-building strategies appropriate for both primary and intermediate students. To help you get the lay of the land, here's a brief logistical outline.

The six chapters in Section 1 zero in on theories related to fluency and explain what fluency is. Chapters 1 and 2 describe the historical trajectory from the round-robin oral reading with which many of us began our careers as readers and reading educators to the idea of "guided oral rereading" and the rationale for its place in a comprehensive reading program. Chapter 3 deals with assessing reading rate: awareness of students' reading rate enables you to plan instruction that moves them beyond the laborious, word-by-word reading so defeating to intermediate readers. Chapters 4 and 5 outline the critical roles of independent reading and teacher "reading prompts" in strengthening readers' fluency. Chapter 6 discusses assessment and how you can use rubrics and fluency checks to monitor readers' fluency and expression.

The remainder of the book provides practical applications (grouped into categories) for dealing with everyday fluency problems—nineteen different techniques, along with numerous variations, that when used correctly over time will increase students' reading fluency. Each strategy includes ways to connect the work with students' life outside school and offers practical suggestions for using it with English language learners. Because it is important that students read authentically and attend to meaning in the process of becoming fluent readers, we also suggest appropriate literature to use with each strategy.

Although each of the techniques has been used successfully in classrooms, you don't need to use each one in yours. The weaknesses and strengths of your students dictate which techniques will be effective. (Figure 6–3 on page 43 and inside front cover, is a quick reference for matching a fluency problem with a recommended technique.)

Section 2 focuses on collaboration and the social aspects of reading that help to build fluency and increase comprehension. Echo reading and shared reading are appropriate for students who need confidence and recognize few words. In both techniques the teacher has a great deal of input and the students are more dependent. When students are able to recognize more words within chosen texts, it is time for collaborative and choral reading. In these two techniques, students are more independent, helping one another through collaboration.

Section 3 focuses on performance. The techniques offered here build confidence as well as fluency, helping students with their expression and rate of reading. Lack of confidence is evidenced in many ways: being unwilling to attempt to decode unknown words, never volunteering to read, or reading so softly we struggle to hear. Fluency flexors involve a great amount of teacher direction and are most appropriate for the more disfluent students. Poetry and readers theatre let students who are getting better at word recognition practice reading smoothly, with greater expression and more confidence. Getting into character, readers theatre, and plays support students' expressive reading. When this expression extends into portraying a character's feelings, it also helps develop inferential skills.

The strategies in Section 4 propel students further in their journey toward independent, fluent reading, although each strategy begins with teacher–student collaboration. Environmental print, although practiced independently, is most effective when created by teacher and students together. Text signals must be explicitly discussed and modeled before students use them independently. Although writing may begin with a teacher-presented minilesson, word walls and print-rich environments support students' independent writing. Repeated readings focus on reading rate but should be explained first and then closely monitored. Children's literature/series books and humorous texts motivate and engage students in their reading. You can hook your students on this kind of material through read-alouds, guided reading, and book talks.

The techniques in Section 5 strengthen students' ability to recognize words rapidly, decode unknown words encountered in context, and more clearly grasp the meanings of individual words. The ideas offered here benefit students far more than a "word drill": they motivate student learning and help them make connections that will increase their comprehension. Sorting words and chunking words support students who need more practice in recognizing words quickly and knowing what they mean. Chunking phrases, like fluency flexors, helps students increase their reading rate by helping them move beyond word-by-word reading. Reading the phrases expressively also deepens comprehension.

Implications for English Language Learners

In proposing a framework for language acquisition, Cummins (2001) outlines three areas on which to focus: meaning, language, and use. For English language learners this means:

1. What they are hearing and reading must be understandable.

2. They must be aware of language forms (semantics, syntax, and orthographic cueing systems) and how they are used.

3. They must be aware of how to use these language forms to create meaning and interpretively read and reread text.

McCauley and McCauley (1992) identify four important elements that help learners acquire a second language. They are (1) a low-anxiety environment, (2) repeated opportunities to practice, (3) comprehensible input, and (4) activities involving drama.

All learners need and deserve an environment characterized by trust and respect. Repeated practice gives learners the time and experience they need to be successful. All learners, but especially those learning English, must be able to understand instruction—what the teacher says and what she expects. Teachers of English language learners speak carefully, clearly, and specifically, checking frequently to make sure students understand. They present material in a number of ways and accompany oral directions with visual supports whenever possible. Introducing drama activities "enables the learner to use language in a social setting . . . (and to) make connections between speech and actions" (Opitz & Rasinski

1998). Providing time for things like choral reading, readers theatre, and plays enables English language readers, through practice and rehearsal, to present performances that are fluent, expressive, and successful.

Text structures are unfamiliar territory for many readers, especially those who are learning to think, read, and write in English as their second language. When first faced with a textbook, many learners have no background or experience with the context or the content, whether it be history, science, or another subject. Helping English language learners—and all students—build background knowledge through discussion, read-alouds, and actual experiences allows all readers to participate fully in all literate pursuits. Giving English language learners opportunities to "preread" a text by discussing concepts, ideas, and structures such as signal words and topic sentences helps build a background of subject matter, syntax, and vocabulary. Experiencing words, phrases, and language structures in a variety of contexts also helps strengthen English language learners' reading comprehension.

Theory
and
Explanation

Fluent Reading

1

What it is fluency? How does it sound? How do we recognize it? Everyone probably defines fluency somewhat differently—there is no one, single accepted definition in the research literature (Fountas & Pinnell 2001). Using the work of many researchers and that of our own combined sixty-plus years as reading educators, we define truly fluent reading as reading that expresses the reader's understanding of the author's message and tone. Much more than fast, accurate reading, truly fluent reading conveys the reader's understanding of content through expressive, interpretive reading of text.

▪ Putting Faces on What Fluency Is Not

Nick's Story

Baffled by her "strongest reader's" poor comprehension on a spring reading assessment, a third-grade teacher asks the building reading teacher to read with Nick. First, the specialist asks Nick to read a third-grade text silently. He reads quickly, but is unable to retell or answer a single literal or inferential question. She then asks him to read another third-grade text aloud. Although he reads with little expression, he has ninety-eight percent accuracy and uses appropriate phrasing and pacing. Again he is unable to retell and answers only one inferential comprehension question correctly. Because both passages are nonfiction, the teacher asks if he prefers fiction. He shrugs and says, "I read both."

This scenario is repeated with two less challenging narrative texts, again one read silently, the other aloud. The results are the same; Nick recalls little and can answer no more than a few comprehension questions.

Following the oral reading, the specialist says, "I've noticed that you are a fast, accurate reader." Nick nods, she smiles. "I also notice that when we try to talk about what you've read, you have trouble remembering." Another nod. "Do you have any idea why that is? What are you thinking about when you read?"

Nick stares at her for several seconds, then launches into a detailed description about a movie he has seen the previous weekend, explaining that he has been replaying the movie in his mind while reading. When she asks why, he says, "Reading's boring, especially the stuff we read at school. Thinking about movies helps me read faster and get done."

In researching Nick's background, the reading teacher discovers that his previous school, in both kindergarten and first grade, used a highly scripted program that included phonetically controlled "practice texts" as the primary reading material. The program, characterized by hours of whole-class instruction in letters and sounds, left little time or opportunity for children to read independently or instructionally in real text (stories and expository texts using literary language).

Josh's Story

Josh, a second grader, reads from a book about robins. He is doing research for a report he will write and present in late November, the culminating project of a fall study of birds and migration. His teacher sits beside him, inquiring about how the research is going and if he is finding what he needs. He shakes his head and says, "There's nothing here about what I wanna know," pointing to a graphic organizer with categories of information to fill in—habitat, food, nesting habits, enemies, interesting or unusual facts. She suggests they read a little together and see what they can find out. He begins, reading in a singsong, halting fashion, his voice rising at the beginning, middle, and end of each sentence, with little regard for phrasing or punctuation. When it is the teacher's turn, she reads with exaggerated but appropriate expression, hoping the modeling will help. When it's Josh's turn again, the singsong persists.

Several pages later they pause and the teacher asks if Josh can use any of the information they have read so far. He takes notes on his graphic organizer, using several bits of information concerning nesting and habitat from the sections the teacher has read. He uses nothing from the part he has read, an interesting section about the robin's eating habits and migratory patterns. As he begins reading again, she stops him and asks why he raises and lowers his voice so often. He replies, "It's more exciting. 'Cause then you wanna hear what the next word is."

Carly's Story

It is late spring and Carly, a first grader, sits with her partner, Rachel, reading aloud from *Frog and Toad Are Friends* (Lobel 1970). Carly has read other Frog and Toad stories, but this one is unfamiliar and she reads carefully, pointing to each word as she progresses slowly down the page. The girls are taking turns, reading alternate pages. When it is Rachel's turn, she reads with expression and intonation and the girls laugh about Toad's behavior. When Carly reads, both girls are serious and silent, Rachel's attention often wandering to those seated around them.

As their teacher is reasonably certain that *Frog and Toad Are Friends* is a "just-right book" (Hoyt 2000) for Carly and therefore one she should be able to read independently, she moves closer, waiting for a chance to intervene. As Rachel's turn ends and the girls turn the page together, the teacher suggests that Carly try to read without her finger. Carly shrugs and moves the finger to the side of the book. Immediately, her reading becomes smoother and more expressive.

◼ Fluency Versus Accuracy

Nick, Josh, and Carly are all disfluent in their own way. Although on the surface they are capable, accurate readers, the ability to make meaning has broken down for them with confusing and frustrating consequences.

In our thirty years of teaching, we have met many "word callers"—readers who scratch the surface, saying the words with only superficial understanding—but none as successful as Nick at divorcing the act of reading from thinking. Although Nick is an extreme, possessed of an uncanny ability to perform multiple tasks simultaneously, he is also a poster child for word calling run amuck. He has mastered what decodable or phonetically controlled text teaches—saying the words accurately and speedily with little concern for meaning.

The Merriam-Webster definition of *fluent* is "capable of flowing: fluid," and Nick's reading could certainly be described as flowing and fluid. However, if reading is first and foremost about making meaning, Nick is not fluent. He has broken the visual code, but semantically he needs immediate help or he will begin to falter and fall behind as reading-to-learn tasks increase.

Much the same is true for Josh. Researching a topic should be engaging, engrossing, and satisfying, answering children's questions and sparking further interest. Josh appears to be focused on the individual words. As a reader, he is not anticipating the meaning, but the next word. Saying the word, making the word more interesting and exciting, are his most important goals. The word, divorced from the context, defines reading for him.

And what about Carly? Frog and Toad's adventures are meant to be laughed at, giggled at, and cried over. She can't do that with her attention and energy spent concentrating on her finger as it isolates the words as individual units.

■ Why Fluency Matters

Based partially on research examining reading fluency of fourth graders (Pinnell et al. 1995), the National Reading Panel (2000) found that "44 percent of students [were] disfluent even with grade-level stories that the students had read under supportive testing conditions" (3–1). This study also found "a close relationship between fluency and reading comprehension" (3–1). The conclusions are obvious—disfluent readers, even those with well-developed phonics and word recognition skills, struggle to make meaning from what they read.

According to a panel of reading experts assembled by the National Center for Education and the Economy (1999), fluency is defined as "the ability to read aloud with appropriate intonations and pauses indicating that students understand the meaning, with only an occasional need to stop to figure out words or sentence structures" (21). This definition situates fluency at the heart of making meaning, highlighting the strong relationship between fluency and reading comprehension. When children read accurately, they read words; when they read for meaning, they comprehend.

Fluent readers recognize that punctuation, sentence structure, and word placement convey meaning. Fluent readers adjust pacing, intonation, phrasing, and expression to convey meaning to listeners or to their own "listening ear." Fluent readers "sing stories" to the author's tune, rather than simply saying the words to complete a task. Fluent readers make text-to-self, text-to-text, and text-to-world connections (Keene & Zimmerman 1997; Harvey & Goudvis 2000) because they are interacting with text, not simply skimming the surface.

■ Developmental Implications Related to Fluency

Fluency develops grade by grade. Kindergartners may reread a familiar story, mimicking their teacher's voice as they pay attention to intonation, phrasing, and expression. Occasionally they point to indicate that they understand that print controls what is said. Fluent first and second graders use intonation, pauses, and emphasis when they read, signaling that they understand that sentence structure implies meaning and that punctuation marks represent guides to meaning (National Center for Education and the Economy 1999).

Intermediate students in grades 3 through 5 read texts of increasing complexity with active, transactional fluency, using many guideposts and structural cues to comprehend. They are expected to make active and thoughtful use of textual information when speaking and writing. In order to be fluent, intermediate readers must be aware of the challenges and supports of varying text structures, using this knowledge to stay meaningfully engaged with text.

▓ Instructional Implications Related to Fluency

The good news—fluency is easy and fun to teach! By participating in the focused, explicit minilessons described in this book, children like Nick, Josh, and Carly are encouraged to interact more actively with text. As they engage in what Calkins (2001) calls deep work with short passages of text, children are helped to recognize the guideposts, pay attention to structural cues, and sing to the author's tune in ways that will strengthen reading comprehension and increase motivation and enjoyment of reading, both out loud and silently.

Teachers want and need manageable strategies to strengthen students' comprehension. They rarely ask specifically for fluency strategies, but when they describe their students' behavior, it often appears that children's lack of engagement and interaction with text centers around fluency issues.

From speedy word callers like Nick, who accurately read whole stories while thinking of something else, to the Joshes and Carlys, with their singsong, choppy, or halting reading habits, readers' disfluency hinders comprehension. Teachers must therefore help them take the next step—to let go of old habits, cease their roles as bystanders, and begin questioning and transacting with text as active participants.

▓ Fluency Centers

Establishing a fluency center in the classroom keeps this aspect of reading in the forefront of students' thinking and provides time and space for students to practice and refine their skills independently. Tape recorders and electronic computer software (*Portfolio Assessment Toolkit* [1994] is just one example) allow students to listen to and assess their own reading. These recordings and e-files can be saved to show progress over time.

■ Connections Between Classroom and Home

One way to bring fluency to caregivers' attention is to ask them to make a monthly recording of their child's reading. These recordings help parents recognize and monitor their child's reading progress and offer appropriate, timely support. It is important to provide careful guidelines:

- Text read should be "easy," with few words that the child cannot read.

- The child should be allowed to read silently first.

- The child should be able to retape as many times as he likes.

Oral Reading

2

The Literacy Dictionary (Harris & Hodges 1995) defines round-robin reading as "the outmoded practice of calling on students to read orally, one after the other" (222). Many people's strongest recollections about reading in school are of doing so in small groups, round-robin style. Turns were taken sequentially around the table; sometimes the readers stood while they read. "Popcorn reading" was much the same, except the teacher called on readers randomly instead of sequentially. Sometimes the reading groups had names like "bluebirds" or "starlings" and occupied particular places in the classroom reading hierarchy. The composition of the groups seldom changed—once a bluebird, always a bluebird. And life as a starling was never fun.

Did people like round-robin oral reading? Well, some loved reading aloud, since it gave them a chance to show everyone how good they were at it. Others remember it as torture, the few most dreaded minutes of the school day. As a shy first grader, Mary Lee spent every school night devising illnesses dire enough to persuade her mother to keep her home, thereby allowing her to avoid reading group. For struggling readers, the agony of forced, unrehearsed reading of unfamiliar text is excruciating, exposing reading weaknesses and uncertainties for all the world to see.

Sadly, round-robin reading is still widely used (Hoffman 1987), mostly because "teachers have not been given many viable alternatives" (Rasinski 2003). In many schools, teachers are not yet familiar with shared or guided reading, both of which are supportive instructional strategies for small-group work.

Teachers may also find independent reading too messy, a too-challenging context in which to track readers' progress.

■ What's So Bad About Round-Robin Reading?

In *Good-Bye Round Robin: Twenty-five Effective Oral Reading Strategies* (Opitz & Rasinski 1998), the authors ask, "Why move away from round-robin reading?" (6). Why indeed. Certainly, it is a practice still widely used in classrooms. So what's wrong with round-robin reading, anyway? It may be a little nerve-racking, but hey, it gives children practice reading aloud and in public. On the surface, it also seems to help teachers keep track of children's progress. Both of these things are true, but there are better, more supportive ways for children to read orally than taking turns reading short segments of text in small, leveled reading groups. Problems with round-robin reading include:

1. It is an unrehearsed, unnatural way to read, particularly in a first encounter with a text. How often are we, as mature readers, asked to read something we have never laid eyes on to a group whose members will be checking every word as we read, ready to jump in and correct us when we falter or make a mistake? When we know we will be called upon to read aloud, we try to practice ahead of time.

2. It may promote inattention and an inaccurate view of reading (Opitz & Rasinski 1998). When adults read aloud to a group, it is usually to convey specific information, not to slog through a passage selected by someone else.

3. For many readers, it is torture. Reading should never be torture, not for anyone, at any time.

4. Readers don't attend to the meaning of the text. They often look ahead, anticipating their section, paying little or no attention to the content or substance of what is read. If they attend at all, they are usually checking another reader's accuracy.

5. The time any one child spends reading is very short. Round-robin readers spend most of their time listening to the reading of others—which is often disfluent and choppy—when they could be reading real, whole texts either during a teacher-supported guided reading lesson or during independent reading.

6. It promotes bad reading habits. Each reader is asked to read word by word; his classmates, reading along silently, are also reduced to reading word by word, often subvocalizing in order to maintain their place.

■ Moving Beyond Round-Robin Reading

Children often choose familiar texts for the sheer joy of playful, expressive re-reading (Griffin 2000). Repeated reading in manageable texts—texts at students' instructional level—builds fluency at every stage of development (Dahl & Samuels 1974; Allington 1983; Dowhower 1987; Rasinski 1989; Zutell & Rasinski 1991; Reutzel & Hollingsworth 1993; Opitz & Rasinski 1998). Oral reading allows children to make important connections between spoken and written language, particularly if it is done using texts and materials that are meant to be read aloud, such as plays, poems, familiar stories, jokes, and songs. Rehearsed oral reading or "guided oral rereading," in which children reread a passage the teacher has just modeled for them, builds reader confidence by smoothing out the process and making it more fluent. Guided oral rereading also helps readers, especially English language learners, make connections to the other language arts—listening, speaking, and writing—while developing and supporting their vocabulary acquisition and reading comprehension (Opitz & Rasinski 1998).

■ How Is Guided Oral Rereading Different from Round-Robin Reading?

The name says it all—readers are guided and they reread text with which they are already familiar. Although there are many models of guided oral rereading, a few key characteristics include:

1. It is rehearsed: children have had previous exposure to the text through teacher read-alouds or their own reading. The emphasis is on practice and making reading better, not exposing errors; having many opportunities to reread makes reading smoother.

2. It is appealing and designed for success. When children read, reread, practice, and perform text, whether together or alone, they experience what it feels like and sounds like to read fluently, to read successfully, to "do it like a reader."

3. It uses books and materials meant to be read aloud. Teachers choose texts that lend themselves to repeated readings—poems, plays, and stories (like *Chicken Aren't the Only Ones* [Heller 1981]) in which words and phrases roll off the tongue in rollicking rhyme and lyrical prose.

4. It builds children's language, vocabulary, and background knowledge by exposing them to different genres of text with increasing complexity. This is especially important for English language learners.

5. It is fun for all students, not just the strongest readers. All children appreciate and enjoy reading successfully. All children deserve this opportunity.

Guided oral rereading supports fluency through its sustained focus on reading as a smooth, meaning-making process. When we hear children reading disfluently, a simple remedial step to take is to pause and suggest a reread, guided or solo. Almost everyone's reading is smoothed the second time through. If not overused or used in such a way that children feel embarrassed or put on the spot, rereading can be a supportive, simple means of focusing children's attention on fluency.

Most of the strategies in this book rely on a form of rereading to build fluency. Choral reading, shared reading, getting into character, fluency flexors, echo reading, radio reading, readers theatre, and collaborative reading all involve some rereading. In addition, whenever we ask young children to "read the room," they are rereading familiar texts through which we have previously guided them.

Reading Rate

3

lthough the scene took place twenty years ago, it seems like yesterday and could be tomorrow. Nancy was teaching Effective Reading 101, a course for college freshmen intended to help them succeed in college and increase their reading speed. The room was filled with machines touted to produce faster, more accurate reading and with young adults needing that skill. One machine, affectionately called the T-scope, was designed like a film projector, except that the screen was inside the machine and the film contained text that would move at a pace set by the instructor. Once a student could read a passage at a given instructional level and answer questions about it, the machine's speed was increased. A second machine, a shadow-scope reader, would light up certain lines of the text as a guide to force the reader to move his eyes faster down the page. As with the T-scope, the shadow-scope reader speed was controllable and could be set fast enough to challenge the speed of the reader.

Evelyn Wood, Nancy was not, but somehow these machines did seem, at least temporarily, to help hundreds of students increase their reading speed. Usually students were initially able to double their reading rate; over time, they probably retained about half of the speed gained. Did this make them better readers? Not better, but perhaps faster for a period of time. Did they comprehend better? Not from using the machines, but perhaps through other strategies and techniques that were taught in the course.

The machines focused on the "mechanics" of student reading. Comprehension is the focus of effective instruction. As new methods became popular, the machines found homes in storage closets. Now, they are being dusted off and are resurfacing, can be ordered on-line, or are being replaced with computer programs that allow text speed to be controlled.

Of course, expensive machines are not the answer. Students can control their own reading speed through internalized techniques and strategies without jeopardizing comprehension. Self-monitoring strategies tell students when they need to slow their reading down or speed it up. Chunking phrases encourages readers to go beyond slow word-by-word reading and take in text through meaningful units. Students also need to be encouraged to abandon tools that slow them down. As children improve in fluency, the rate of reading increases.

▤ Why Is Reading Speed Important?

Reading rate and accuracy are parts of fluency. As Richard Allington points out in *What Really Matters for Struggling Readers* (2001), practice is a powerful contributor to the development of accurate, fluent, high-comprehension reading. According to Allington, students at every age level who read more pages than others in school and for homework each day had higher NAEP reading scores (27). When a student cannot read at a reasonable rate we need to focus on two things: (1) the decoding that is interfering with comprehension and (2) the amount of reading.

Students who read faster, read more. If student A reads ten pages during fifteen minutes of SSR and student B reads twenty, student B is obviously reading twice as much. In a 180-day academic year, student A will have read 1,800 pages, student B, 3,600 pages. To translate that into books, let's use *Chasing Redbird,* by Sharon Creech (1997), which is 260 pages, as a guide. On average, student A will read seven books during the school year, while student B will read fourteen. If this reading discrepancy—during just fifteen minutes of every day—continues from grade 4 to the end of high school, student B will have read approximately *sixty-three more books* than student A. Reading rate matters.

▤ What Influences Reading Rate?

For savvy readers, the obvious answer to this question is *purpose*. People read at different rates for different purposes. Various factors influence how fast a student is reading, not how fast a student can read. The attraction of using technology, such as the T-scope, to gain reading speed is not the technology itself but what it forces the reader to do: decrease the number of eye fixations (stops) per line by increasing eye span. In essence, as long as students are not having problems with automaticity, if they can pick up more words at a time in fewer "stops" per line, they will increase their reading speed—but not necessarily their comprehension.

Students should not gain reading speed at the cost of comprehension. On the other hand, they may be reading so slowly they can't decipher or hold on to the meaning of the text. Experts continue to "sit on the fence" in relation to reading rate: students need to read as fast as they can without interfering with comprehension. Reading strategies offered in this book such as phrase sorts, fluency flexors, chunking, and words-in-context work to increase eye span while still focusing on comprehension.

Teachers shouldn't start counting eye fixations, but they do need to monitor students' reading rate. If a student's rate of reading is interfering with her comprehension and self-esteem or causing a problem with academic work in general, then strategies that develop fluency—and therefore increase reading rate—need to be employed.

■ What Is a Reasonable Reading Rate?

Reading rate is affected by a variety of factors: purpose for reading, difficulty and nature of content, text format, and sentence structure. Consequently, studies comparing reading rates are problematic (Harris & Hodges 1995). A number of studies have focused on average words per minute (WPM); others use words correct per minute (WCPM). (It appears that accuracy is assumed when WPM is used; also, in silent reading, accuracy can't be determined and WPM is the only way to count words read.) Some charts offer one expected norm for silent reading, another for oral reading. The bottom line: scientific studies vary greatly in the expected reading rate they determine to be appropriate for particular grade levels.

The two charts offered here (Figures 3–1 and 3–2, pp. 16–17) sum up the results of eight studies of reading rates. The material and approach in these studies vary as greatly as the range of the rates given. For instance, Carver (1989) used different passages to accommodate individual reading levels, while Hasbrouck and Tindal (1992) had all students at a grade level read the same text. In the latter case, the passage read would most likely have been at an independent level for some readers, yet at the frustration level for others.

The next-to-the-last column in each table is an "average" score for the four studies: we added the median (middle) scores for each range given and averaged them to find the mean. The last column in each table offers a goal rate for

GRADE	POWELL	HANSBROUCK & TINDAL	LESLIE & CALDWELL	RICHEK, LIST & LEARNER	AVERAGE	TARGET
1	45–65	—	31–87	—	57	71
2	70–100	82–104	52–102	70–100	85	100
3	105–125	107–142	85–139	95–130	116	121
4	125–145	125–143	78–124	120–170	126	141
5	135–155	126–151	—	160–210	156	163
6	140–160	171–200	113–165	180–230	170	—

FIG. 3–1 *Oral Reading: Expected Rates (WPM)*

students to strive for: it's that grade level's average rate combined with the average rate for the grade level above. This target rate is approximately the WPM that students should be reading by the end of that year and the beginning of the next.

(An aside here: research indicates that economically disadvantaged students tend to return to school in September with diminished reading skills, whereas economically advantaged students tend to improve—modestly—their reading skills [Allington and McGill-Franzen 2003]. That being the case, some students may never start the school year with the expected rate of reading for their grade level.)

■ How Is Reading Rate Calculated?

The easiest and most common technique used to calculate WPM is to have a child read for exactly one minute and then count the words. (After one minute of reading, have the child point at the word she has reached.) If your concern is where the child stands in relation to the average rate, before you have him read put a light mark near the word that matches the average number for his grade level. For example, if the child is a second grader and he is reading silently, put a light mark by the ninety-fifth word. On a record sheet the marks −, √, or + can represent below, at, or above average, respectively.

Words per minute can also be calculated by using the following formula:

$$\text{WPM} = \frac{(\# \text{ of words read}) \times (60 \text{ sec/min})}{\# \text{ of seconds child read}}$$

GRADE	ALLINGTON	POWELL	LESLIE & CALDWELL	CARVER	AVERAGE	TARGET
1	60–90	45–65	—	81	57	76
2	85–120	70–100	58–122	82–108	95	111
3	115–140	120–140	96–168	109–130	128	138
4	140–170	130–180	107–175	131–147	148	161
5	170–195	165–205	—	148–161	174	183
6	195–220	190–220	135–241	162–174	192	—

FIG. 3–2 *Silent Reading: Expected Rates (WCPM)*

▦ The Bottom Line

The importance of a child's rate of reading should never supercede the need for adequate comprehension. Savage (1994) states that unless the rate is inordinately slow, reading rate should not be of primary importance. Studies, however, do suggest that faster rates of reading correlate to higher comprehension (Allington 2001) and that reading rate is a good predictor of general reading achievement (Rasinski 1999). The consensus seems to be that if a child's reading rate is so slow that it hinders her reading comprehension or interferes with her motivation to read, then steps need to be taken to increase the child's reading rate.

Students should be encouraged to strive for their personal best. Dedicated runners spend hundreds of dollars a year to run races they know they will not win. Their objective is not to win the race, but to challenge themselves and run a new personal best. They plan to enjoy the race. They go out with confidence and keep running at a pace that is demanding but not harmful. They slow down when the demands of running fast might interfere with their objective of finishing the race.

A number of strategies in this text can help increase reading rate, such as having student reread familiar text until they are comfortable with it and having older students time themselves as a motivator to increase reading speed. Teachers are personal trainers. They need to insist that their students do their "personal best." The trick is to keep your students at a reading rate that is challenging but not uncomfortable. You never want them to lose sight of their main objective: constructing meaning from print.

4 | Independent Reading

Ⅰt's often said but bears repeating: children are not empty pails waiting for teachers to fill them up with knowledge. They are not blank slates when they enter the classroom, but persons with rich, diverse lives, individuals who bring unique backgrounds and experiences to their school communities. In order to become competent readers and writers, these individuals require direct instruction. They also need time in which to read, the opportunity to choose what they will read, and texts that are at appropriate levels if we expect them to become fluent, competent, confident readers.

■ The Gift of Time

Fluent readers need time to practice reading independently every day. It sounds so simple—if we want students to be stronger readers, we must give them time to read. As readers apply the reading skills and strategies we teach them, they learn new words and meanings, strengthen their word-solving skills, and internalize an understanding of story themes and text structures. Unbelievably, it is the very act of reading that is being crowded out or neglected in the current push for scripted programs and direct instruction. Independent reading, SSR (sustained silent reading), and D.E.A.R. (Drop Everything and Read)—opportunities for readers to apply skills and strategies learned during direct instruction—have been supplanted by hours of phonics and phonemic awareness activities. Then, if and when there is time to read, students are given decodable texts, "controlled" to include only those sounds and word patterns learned during direct instruction. Given scenarios like these, how are students ever to become fluent, confident readers?

Readers improve by reading (Anderson, Wilson & Fielding 1988). Period. In examining time spent reading in relation to reader competency, research points to enormous differences in the amount of time children spend reading. By the middle grades, the least engaged, least competent readers have read approximately 100,000 words; the average reader, 1,000,000 words; and the most involved, most motivated readers, 10,000,000 to 50,000,000 words (Nagy & Anderson 1984). This gap is enormous and has a huge impact on readers' competencies, engagement, confidence, and fluency.

■ The Ability to Choose

Fluent readers read for a reason and choose reading materials that interest them. Readers problem-solve their way through text fueled by curiosity about the world and the stories it contains. In real texts that engage their minds and hearts, readers have many opportunities to apply skills and strategies. We have yet to meet a reader whose mind or heart was engaged or touched by "Nan ran to fan the man." Our children deserve better. They also deserve the right—with guidance—to make decisions about what they will read. Children in classrooms in which they are allowed to make choices about reading and writing read better and more often than children in classrooms that do not allow such autonomy (Anderson, Wilson, & Fielding 1988).

■ Leveled Texts

The concept of instructional text—reading a more challenging text with the guidance and support of the teacher or a more capable peer—is related to Vygotsky's (1978) theory of zones of proximal development. When matching books to readers for instructional activities such as guided reading, teachers aim for just-right books that provide a few challenges. Just-right books provide opportunities for teaching, coaching, modeling, and learning during guided reading.

When readers read independently, however, they do not have an adult or capable peer at their side to help them. Therefore, students should be able to read these texts without assistance. Because our aim is to develop fluency, just-right independent books may present a few opportunities for problem solving, but by and large they should flow easily.

Establishing Criteria

Let's look at this Goldilocks strategy of book selection (Ohlhausen & Jepsen 1992) a bit more carefully. Just as Goldilocks in the familiar folktale searched for the just-right porridge, chair, and bed, readers can search for books that are either "too easy," "too hard," or "just right":

- *Texts that are too hard* present many challenges for the reader, challenges that prevent fluent reading and ultimately defeat the child's efforts to process and understand. Depending on grade level and reader competence, too-hard texts often have smaller, hard-to-decipher print or less "white space" than readers prefer. They also have many unfamiliar words and few illustrations.

- *Texts that are too easy* have probably been read many times. Readers toss them off fluently, often "without looking," as first graders say.

- *Texts that are just right* may have a few tricky parts, but in general they are texts that readers are able to read and enjoy easily. Just-right texts are also those that children want to read, texts that interest and excite them, texts that motivate them to read on, strengthening fluency and skills.

Variations of the Goldilocks strategy can be used by teachers and students in grades K–5. What is critical is to develop selection criteria *with the students*. Teachers need to introduce and discuss this book selection strategy, then demonstrate, model, and discuss criteria for all three types of texts. Children should be given opportunities to analyze texts, help determine criteria, and choose books based on those criteria. The criteria for each type of text can be published in a number of ways, including:

- *Charts* posted prominently on classroom walls and to which teachers refer frequently. These charts can be changed and added to as readers gain confidence and practice choosing just-right texts.

- *Just-right bookmarks* listing the criteria. These can be decorated by students and laminated.

- *Just-right strategy cards* listing the criteria. These, too, can be decorated by students and laminated.

Finding Books

Once students have developed criteria for text selection, where do they go to find just-right texts? Well-organized classroom libraries assist readers in locating the books they need. One of Mary Lee's first reading minilessons of the year, no matter whether teaching kindergarten or fifth grade, is to take her students on a tour of the classroom library, discussing where to find things and how to treat books and spaces.

There are many ways to display just-right texts in a classroom:

- Browsing boxes (or some other organizational unit) containing books at levels just below readers' instructional level.

- Students' published books (often the most valuable reading material in the classroom).

- Familiar books (read previously during instruction and/or with a partner).

- Charts, poems, and stories written as a class and posted around the classroom for students to reread.

- New versions of a familiar folk- or fairy tale.

- Books with accompanying tapes on which the oral reader reads slowly enough for a silent reader to follow along. (There are computer "books" of this kind, but students are then staring at a computer screen, not holding a book or a piece of paper. Nice for a change, but not recommended as a steady diet.)

Many teachers say, "This all sounds great but I don't have the books." And it's true, some classrooms have hundreds of books, others only a handful. Some schools have extensive leveled book collections or literacy closets, others don't. Although it's important continually to build school leveled collections and classroom libraries, we needn't throw up our hands if independent reading choices are not at our fingertips. Putting the right book in the right child's hand at the right moment is some of the most important work we do, and we must continually seek out sources. Here are a few suggestions:

- ***Make friends with your local librarian.*** Most public libraries will allow teachers to take fifty books or more for extended times.

- ***Create lots of text with students.*** Language-experience stories, interactive and modeled writing, and children's free writing can be posted around the room. This can also be "published" in book form and put on the library shelves for independent reading.

- ***Start a book drive*** or book donation program in which families or community members donate books. Every year wonderful books are donated to church and library book sales. These books could be donated to classrooms just as easily. It never hurts to ask!

- *Make friends with a publishing sales rep.* When we are at conferences and workshops, striking up a conversation with a sales representative will frequently result in a free book or two, either on the spot or later by mail. And we *always* ask about discounts.

- *Start a letter-writing campaign* outlining a school's or classroom's need for books. Children are often the best spokespeople for these kinds of campaigns, and local businesses are sometimes happy to donate funds or books

- *Yard sales* are often treasure troves of children's books; it takes only a few minutes to pull over when you see a sale in progress.

- *Books clubs,* and their familiar monthly newsletters that can drive one a little nutty, are great sources of "free" books. For every order, the classroom usually receives at least one or two books, and 1000 points equals 100 books!

■ Structuring Independent Reading Time

Whether you call it SSR, D.E.A.R., or one of the many other designators for independent reading, how you structure the time is important. It may be more appropriate to consider independent reading as a "workshop" in which students think, conjecture, problem-solve, create, and share. We recommend forty-five to sixty minutes, very similar in shape and design to a writing workshop, beginning with a minilesson, followed by sustained reading, and ending with whole-group sharing. Obviously, the bulk of the time is devoted to actual reading.

1. *Minilesson:* A brief lesson (five or ten minutes) outlining a skill or strategy readers can then apply to their reading. Many of the strategies in the rest of this book can be presented as minilessons.

2. *Sustained reading:* A sustained period of twenty to forty minutes (or longer!) during which individuals read on their own (or sometimes with a partner). The teacher circulates, conferring and checking in. (See the coaching prompts in Chapter 5 for ideas about conferring with independent readers.)

3. *Sharing:* Five or ten minutes in which the class gathers and readers share something about their reading. Such sharing could focus on fluency, comprehension, vocabulary, word solving, or another aspect of reading. Often

sharing relates back to the skill or strategy introduced during the mini-lesson. Sharing with one another is just as important in reading workshop as it is in writing workshop.

■ Matching Books to Readers

As they are learning and applying new skills and strategies, readers at every level need books that provide different kinds of support. There are many excellent resources that describe such supports, like *Matching Books to Readers: Using Leveled Books in Guided Reading, K–3* (Fountas & Pinnell 1999) and *Leveled Books for Readers Grades 3–6* (Pinnell & Fountas 2002). The following brief considerations will help you develop libraries for primary and intermediate readers.

Our Development of Fluency Chart (Figure 4–1) has been adapted from many sources including the *Reading and Writing Grade by Grade: Primary Literacy Standards for Kindergarten Through Grade 3* (National Center for Education and the Economy 1999) as well as our own work with students and teachers of all grade levels. As Figure 4–1 illustrates, the nature of fluency changes as children progress as readers. They select different kinds of text, which may sound quite different from one another (think of narrative versus exposition, for example). Although we might very occasionally rhapsodize over something we read in the newspaper, we generally do not read such text in quite the same way we read poetry or lyrical prose.

Failing to take into account reader development and the kind of text readers select ignores critical aspects of fluency. Only by attending to readers' development levels and the challenges of texts they encounter at those levels can we provide appropriate instruction and intervention when readers need them most.

Primary Books

Books scaffold readers in the primary grades in a variety of ways (Prescott-Griffin, 2005). Once familiar with text structures and patterns, readers often zip through predictable text with joyous familiarity (Martin & Brogan 1972). Such books provide literate building blocks and support children's growing literate understanding.

Predictable texts with repetitive language draw readers in, provoking behavior such as rereading, thereby promoting fluency and building reader confidence (Griffin 2000). Predictable texts help readers internalize linguistic patterns that they then draw upon when reading subsequent texts. Predictable patterned texts also increase the number of words children can recognize on

GRADE	WHAT DOES FLUENCY LOOK LIKE?	CHARACTERISTICS OF GRADE-LEVEL TEXTS
K	• Reread favorite or familiar stories with expression and appropriate phrasing. • Point to text, indicating their understanding that print determines what is said (read).	• Simple story lines. • Single concept or idea explored. • Relate to children's personal experiences. • One to three lines to a page (one or two sentences). • Print large, clear, and separated by ample white space (for pointing and word-by-word matching). • Text supported by pictures.
1	• Independently read (aloud or silently) grade-level texts that have been introduced or previewed for them with expression. • Use appropriate phrasing, pauses, and emphasis. • Attend to text signals such as punctuation (commas, periods, question marks) in order to read with meaning and intonation.	• Stories more complex, with several episodes and more sophisticated plot. • Present opportunities for readers to explore new ideas, themes, concepts, and points of view. • Provide sufficient structure and content to make comparisons with other texts. • More pages, more sentences per page, and more unusual, specialized vocabulary. • Unfamiliar or multisyllabic words that challenge their problem-solving abilities. • Simple chapter books such as the Frog and Toad (Lobel) Henry and Mudge (Rylant) series, with full-page illustrations to support text.
2	• Independently read (aloud or silently) grade-level texts that have been introduced or previewed for them with expression. • Use appropriate phrasing, pauses, and emphasis. • Attend to text signals such as punctuation (commas, periods, question marks) in order to read with meaning and intonation.	• Longer chapter books, with fewer illustrations that provide less support for readers. • More complex plots, with multiple characters and well-developed setting, events, and points of view. • Sophisticated language and challenging vocabulary. • Demand deeper level of thinking and reader engagement than lower-level texts. • Require greater inferencing and "reading between the lines" than lower-level texts.
3–5	• Independently read (aloud or silently) grade-level texts that have been introduced or previewed for them with expression, intonation, and phrasing that indicate the meaning of text. • Easily read words with irregular affixes and morphemes (such as *ex, ous, ion, ive*). • Use text signals and cues (punctuation, sentence structure) to assist meaning in increasingly more complex texts. • Use appropriate expression to signify meaning when reading aloud.	• Longer chapter books, novels, informational texts, and textbooks. • Fiction with sophisticated plots that allow readers to explore unfamiliar concepts, ideas, setting, and characters. • Fiction and nonfiction that allow more in-depth reader focus on craft and genre. • Nonfiction texts with more detailed, more sophisticated information—historical, scientific, mathematical, etc.—of which readers may or may not possess background knowledge. • Nonfiction texts with complex and varied structures (compare/contrast, cause and effect, chronological, persuasive, etc.). • Textbooks with many new text signals and structures requiring specialized teaching and study-skills practice.

FIG. 4–1 *Development of Fluency, K–5*

sight. Illustrations in most predictable picture books are closely connected to the words, thus supporting young readers' processing. Some texts use words of familiar children's songs as text. Singable text keeps motivation high as readers negotiate their way through more difficult passages where the text patterns change (Prescott-Griffin 2005).

Primary readers advance from predictable patterned texts to those in which pictures still provide support and print is clear and surrounded by ample white space. Simple chapter books like Lobel's Frog and Toad series and Rylant's Henry and Mudge series fall into this category. They support developing readers' skills and strategies while telling wonderful stories that engage children's hearts and minds.

Some classrooms have a supply of "decodable texts," which focus readers' attention on print at the expense of meaning. Decodable texts reinforce the alphabetic nature of language. If our goals are to build reader fluency and competence, a steady diet of decodable texts is a poor and potentially damaging alternative to matching readers to real texts. In fact, we cringe when we hear recommendations that seventy-five percent of primary students' reading material should be decodable texts. This may be a great way to promote bored word calling, but it is a very poor substitute for engaged, thoughtful reading of real texts.

Intermediate Books

As Figure 4–1 indicates, readers in grades 3 through 5 are encountering more complex stories and textbooks. In building intermediate readers' fluency, series books provide familiar, supportive textual contexts to keep readers coming back for more. Series like Mary Pope Osborn's Magic Tree House books and Dan Greenburg's Zack Files are enormously popular with intermediate readers and often lead them into other series like Tomi De Paola's Fairmont Avenue books.

Intermediate readers often face textbooks for the first time, with their unfamiliar structures, conventions, and content. Although specific minilessons can help students navigate expository texts, having a variety of nonfiction reading materials in classroom libraries builds readers' background knowledge for the time when they are required to read expository texts. Biographies with beautiful photographs and simple text build readers' knowledge of history, and books like Joanna Cole's Magic School Bus series are excellent first exposures to scientific concepts and vocabulary. A beautifully photographed and meticulously researched nonfiction book such as Seymour Simon's (1991) *Earthquakes* engages

readers' interests and introduces concepts and vocabulary they will encounter in
science textbooks later on.

◾ Getting Specific

Once we are aware of readers' disfluent habits, we not only teach, model, and
coach but also help them select books they will want to read, books that will motivate them to read with expression, interest, and joyous abandon. Readers at all
levels deserve access to rich and varied print materials. Teachers of reading must
be active consumers of children's literature, reading great books, visiting libraries
and bookstores, and befriending librarians and others who are knowledgeable
about the literature so that they are always discovering those just-right books
for their readers. What books might interest the disfluent readers we met in
Chapter 1?

Nick

Nick finds reading neither pleasurable nor interesting. It is simply something he
is required to do at school. In order to get through this boring activity, he has de-
vised ways to let his mind wander while still reading the words. He can, if called
upon, complete a book report, sketching out enough details to get by. When he
is asked to read for information and deeper levels of meaning, however, he is
lost. At the same time that we teach and model fluent reading strategies, we
must find texts that interest and engage Nick as much as the movies and videos
he watches constantly when not in school.

Does he respond to humor? Adventure? Would he enjoy reading and solving
a mystery along with Landon's Meg Mackintosh, Sobel's Encyclopedia Brown,
or Brooks' Freddie the Detective? Would he identify and laugh at the antics of
Tom Fitzgerald in the Great Brain series, or Soup in Peck's Soup series? Once we
find a book or series that interests Nick, we will want to give him specific purposes for reading. When asking him to share his reading or write a reading response, we will nudge Nick below the surface, beyond literal thinking, to make
inferences and draw conclusions about what he reads.

Reading and discussing books with a partner or as part of a literature circle
might also be a way to engage Nick more actively during independent reading,
giving him access to the literate understanding of others. Knowing that he has a
responsibility to share with a partner or small group following his silent reading
may provide valuable incentive for Nick to think more carefully and actively
about what he is reading.

Josh

Even though Josh has made the transition to silent reading—his preferred way to read—his singsong, inappropriate phrasing and expression persist as subvocalizations. When he reads silently, he reads word by word, his inner voice rising and falling at odd and inappropriate moments. Josh needs specific purposes for his independent reading, and he needs encouragement to pause often, to monitor comprehension. When he reads independently, we need to check in frequently, asking him to tell us about his reading or read a page aloud to us.

When helping Josh select books, we should take advantage of his interests and steer him toward texts that will engage him. Acquainting him with conventions of nonfiction text and how to read and reread for information will help him approach text in a more purposeful way. Whether he is reading independently or aloud to us, we want him to read for himself—for enjoyment and information—not perform. Because he is a second grader, we want to give him experiences with both fiction and nonfiction texts in preparation for the reading expectations of the grades ahead. Pairing fiction and nonfiction texts makes useful connections for Josh. For example, he could read Mary Pope Osborn's *Afternoon on the Amazon* (1995) with the companion nonfiction text *Rain Forests* (Osborn & Osborn 2001). Such pairings make connections for readers: the same vocabulary, concepts, and situations often appear in both texts.

Carly

Carly is on the verge of fluency in grade-level text. With practice reading independently in books she loves, Carly's skills will strengthen and she will be able to move more flexibly between strategies in processing text. We need to encourage her to read without her finger, to smooth her reading out. We also want to find just-right books that will engage and interest her. Like many first graders, Carly wants to read "chapter" books. Series like Rylant's Henry and Mudge books, Lobel's Frog and Toad books, and Moore Thomas' *Good Night, Good Knight* (2000) are wonderful independent reading choices for Carly. These books have a number of excellent supports for "almost fluent" readers. They are well written, heartwarming, and humorous. The print is large and clear and is surrounded by ample white space. Illustrations support the reader's processing and understanding of the text. Mostly, they are fun—fun to read and fun to share with others. (As adults, the Frog and Toad story entitled "The Swimsuit" still makes us smile with its many truths about friendship, vanity, and human nature.)

When Carly reads independently, frequent teacher "check-ins" will support her efforts at smooth, fluent reading. We want to support her efforts to let go of the finger while not acting too abruptly in removing a form of self-help she has come to rely on. When we sit down beside Carly and notice her finger pointing, we might suggest an interim strategy of running her hand down the page as she reads, encouraging her to save pointing for those times when she encounters an unfamiliar word.

Coaching for Fluency | 5

L iteracy educators' ultimate goal is to produce independent readers and writers by gradually releasing responsibility for reading and writing to the students (Pearson & Gallagher 1983). Reading programs should move from activities like teacher read-alouds and shared reading, characterized by a lot of teacher support and control and little student control, to activities like independent reading, which require less teacher support and feature a great deal of student control (Fountas & Pinnell 1996). As first-grade teacher Kristen Vito says, "We model, model, model, then step back and observe, highlighting the good choices students make. There's lots of positive reinforcement." As teachers gradually turn over responsibility for reading to the students, they continue to coach and support them in all its facets, including fluency, highlighting and celebrating students' independent mastery of literate tasks.

During writing workshop, Calkins (1986) uses minilessons as a scaffold grounded in modeling theory, direct instruction, and developmental theory (Bruner & Ratner 1978; Cazden 1988; Graves 1984). The fluency minilessons in the remaining sections of this book are excellent scaffolds. If, as Fosnot (1996) argues, these minilessons perturb learners, contradicting what they think is good reading behavior, the students will return to reading with new, evaluative perspectives from which to examine their own fluent (or disfluent) behavior. Explicit instruction, coaching, and feedback help readers build fluency skills and strategies (Koskinen & Blum 1986; Rasinski 1989).

You can coach fluency with a whole class, in a small group, or one-on-one, depending on the needs of your readers. The process is to model first, then step back, being sure to check in during independent reading, supporting and celebrating readers' efforts. It's essential to prompt and reteach as needed, provide the appropriate tools, and schedule ample time in which students can practice and reread familiar texts.

Opportunities to revisit familiar text are particularly important, because they allow young readers to experience the feel of fluent, expressive reading instead of always plodding through appropriately challenging text on first or second readings.

■ Teacher Modeling

Daily models of fluent reading include:

- **Reading aloud** from picture books, novels, and other print materials. Hearing many books read aloud helps readers internalize the rhythm and flow of written language, which is very different than spoken language. For all children, especially English language learners, listening to someone reading aloud fluently builds background knowledge about reading: its processes, concepts, and vocabulary.

- **Shared reading,** a model associated with the primary grades in which teachers use big-print stories (big books, or stories copied onto charts) to focus children's attention on print concepts and beginning reading strategies. Shared reading is also an important means of modeling fluent reading and can be effectively used with students in grades K–5. With older students, shared reading focuses readers' attention on "text signals" (punctuation or unusual print treatments such as boldface or italics).

- **Commercial reading programs.** Read Naturally (*www.readnaturally.com*), for example, was developed by Candace Ihnot, a Title I reading specialist, and features fluent models of reading by the teacher (or via tapes), repeated rereadings, and monitoring of reading rate. Students practice and reread passages three or four times along with a tape recording or their teacher and are then monitored by the teacher. Evaluations of Read Naturally by the developers (Hasbrouck, Ihnot, & Rogers 1999) reveal promising results for urban Title I students in the intermediate and middle school grades.

- **Books on tape.** Unfortunately, the pace of reading on most commercially produced recordings is too fast for young readers to follow along. If readers cannot follow, they do not benefit from the opportunity to read along and practice fluency. Eyes-on-text time is compromised. Book recordings read at a pace that allows readers to keep up are available from Marie Carbo (*www.nrsi.com/merchantz*). *Teaching Students to Read Through Their Individual Learning Styles* (Carbo, Dunn, & Dunn 1986) provides instructions for creating appropriately paced recordings for students; the book can be used to train parents and older students to tape books. With a little planning and willing volunteers, schools can create extensive listening libraries of appropriately paced texts to enhance students' fluency and enjoyment of reading. These materials can then be used independently by students in listening or fluency centers.

- **Computer books** for young readers. Living Books (*www.livingbooks.com*) are excellent models of fluent reading and provide instant visual and auditory feedback. If matched to readers, these programs are an interesting, alternative form of fluency practice and reinforcement.

When planning lessons or coaching students on the use of any reading skill or strategy, always keep fluency in mind. When asked if she encourages "buddy readers" to hint before helping their partner over a rough spot, Kristen Vito smiles and says, "They [readers] will use the cueing systems, but there is always the issue of fluency and maintaining the flow of the story." Although she suggests that partners hint rather than take over when their buddy struggles, she also appreciates the enormous importance of fluency in retaining meaning and reader engagement. Kristen's students explain that the strategy they use most when their partner encounters an unfamiliar word in text is to "tell the word" rather than hint. This retains the flow of story and doesn't disrupt the continuity.

An important part of teaching is balancing which strategies and skills are emphasized lesson to lesson. As Kristen and her students demonstrate, this is not always easy or straightforward. Listening is key. Although scaffolding and assistance are important skills to encourage, when reading buddies choose different strategies in order to preserve meaning and fluency, their efforts should be respected and applauded.

■ Fluency Tools

Young readers appreciate and benefit from "reading tools" such as their finger, bookmarks, strategy cards, and charts. An important part of scaffolding involves knowing when to remove a scaffold that is no longer needed. In observing readers, think about when to encourage them to use a tool and when to begin weaning them from tools they no longer need, tools that are slowing them down.

Finger Pointing and Bookmarks

Once readers are able to apply multiple strategies as they read, moving flexibly between semantic, syntactic, and orthographic cueing systems, they may need to be discouraged from using either their finger or a bookmark to keep their place. These tools, essential for many emergent readers in tracking and word-by-word matching, can hinder the "almost-fluent" reader, because they can support subvocalizing and word-by-word reading, slow and inefficient behavior in silent reading. Bookmarks, another popular tool for beginning readers, also sometimes get in the way as readers move toward fluency. Almost-fluent readers should be assessed, to learn if these tools are helping or hindering them.

Reading Phones

When children read aloud with partners and alone, particularly in the primary grades, the resulting cacophony can become a problem. "Reading phones" made from PVC piping (see Figure 5–1) cut down on the noise while still allowing readers to listen to themselves and enhance their awareness of fluency. These inexpensive "elbow pipes" can be found in any building supply store.

FIG. 5–1 *Reading Phones*

Strategy Cards and Charts

Many teachers use cards, bookmarks, and charts to remind children of reading strategies. The best of these tools are created *with children*, using their language and ideas. Strategy cards or charts related to fluency remind readers of the behavior and strategies modeled during direct instruction. The prompts and coaching strategies in the following section are examples.

◼ Fluency Prompts: Coaching Readers on the Run

As you listen to a child read, you have the opportunity to offer relevant, personalized guidance. You can suggest strategies to help her smooth out her reading and support her understanding of what is being read. The following prompts are geared to individuals but may be used in a variety of contexts, including the whole class or a small group. Think of these prompts as just the right idea to use at just the right moment in order to enhance a reader's fluency.

1. ***A reader is not attending to "text signals" such as punctuation or print variations (boldface, capitals, italics):***
   - What does your voice do when you see a period? Question mark? Exclamation mark?
   - Make your voice go down when you see a period, then stop.
   - Make your voice go up when you see a question mark, then stop.
   - Read with excitement when you see an exclamation mark.
   - Take a breath when you see a comma.
   - Show me what your voice does when you see bold print.
   - Show me what your voice does when you see words all in capital letters in the middle of sentences.
   - Show me what your voice does when you see italicized text.

2. ***Reading is slow, halting, or choppy or inappropriately expressive:***
   - Read that part [indicate a phrase or sentence] again quickly.
   - Read this part [indicate a phrase or short sentence] without taking a breath.
   - Listen to me read, then echo the way I did it.
   - Read to me pointing to each word, then take away your finger and read again. Which sounds smoother?

3. *A reader has trouble understanding what he has read:*
   - Read it to help me feel the story.
   - Read it to help me learn.
   - Let me hear the character talking.
   - Read like the author intended.

4. *A reader seems to be unaware of her disfluency:*
   - How does your reading sound?
   - Is your reading rough or smooth?
   - Does the way you're reading help tell the story?
   - Does your reading sound interesting?
   - Will your reading make someone want to listen to see what comes next?

■ Considerations for English Language Learners

A prereading discussion of concepts and vocabulary related to stories and text to be modeled and practiced gives all learners, especially those learning English, background, experience, and conceptual understanding to bring to their reading. When reading and rereading, English language learners benefit from visual prompts or oral or written (on the blackboard, chart paper, or cards) questions related to text.

Providing many opportunities for English language learners to listen to expressive reading, reread the selection themselves, and check their fluency helps them internalize English language rhythms and structures. The activities in this book that support learning new words and their meanings in many contexts are especially important for English language learners. Also, when coaching and prompting English language learners, make connections to and comparisons with the sound and feel of their first language wherever possible.

Assessing Fluency

6

Just as we regularly assess children's reading accuracy and understanding, we should take time regularly to collect meaningful data on their fluency. There are, of course, many commercially produced fluency assessments on the market. But because our purpose is to collect data we can use to inform instruction, it is more relevant to monitor our students' fluency using quality literature and the interesting texts found in school and classroom libraries and book rooms.

You may select or develop whatever reading fluency checklists, rubrics, and assessment scales you find most relevant. Both quantitative and qualitative measures are useful. Assessments of reading rate and accuracy (miscue analysis, etc.), though important, are only part of the picture. Quantitative measures cannot provide critical information about reader interest and motivation. They are also of limited use in assessing comprehension and the connections between reader fluency and understanding.

No matter what fluency assessments you choose, whenever possible *use the texts in which students are learning.* This ensures that both the assessment and the resulting instruction are relevant to what your readers need at this particular time in their particular literacy journey.

Rubrics and Checklists

Rubrics are a way to attend to aspects of fluency such as voice quality, expression, phrasing, attention to text signals (punctuation, capital letters, sentence boundaries, bold and italicized print), and accuracy. Fluency rubrics also provide information about reader understanding and motivation as appropriately expressive reading depends on the reader's interest in and comprehension of text. Smooth, accurate reading is not always accompanied by strong comprehension. Likewise, plodding, tentative reading does not always imply poor comprehension. Many slow readers are nevertheless able to read for meaning. Although we want to help slow readers increase their rate, we also want to reinforce their already well-developed comprehension skills and strategies.

There are many useful fluency rubrics. Linda Hoyt's (2000) Scoring Guide for Fluency and Expression is appropriate for primary readers; Fountas and Pinnell's (1996, p. 81) Rubric for Fluency Evaluation is useful for K–5 readers; and the research-based fluency scale from NAEP's Integrated Reading Performance Record Oral Reading Fluency Scale (Pinnell et al. 1995), although designed for fourth graders, could be adapted for students in grades 3 and 5 as well.

Rubrics, checklists, and other measures of fluency should be easy for teachers to use while listening to students read during guided reading, independent reading, or science or social studies periods. Ideally, some kind of fluency check should take place every four to six weeks. Also, teachers should tape-record each student's reading several times a year, analyze these tapes (preferably in collaboration with their colleagues), and retain them for comparison and documentation. At least once a year, a faculty or planning meeting should focus on fluency, as the teachers analyze and discuss representative tape recordings of student work.

In assessing fluency, we want to be as holistic as possible, examining many dimensions of students' oral reading (Zutell & Rasinski 1991). In creating the Fluency Check, Teacher Version (Figure 6–1), we have adapted and incorporated facets of the NAEP's Integrated Reading Performance Record Oral Reading Fluency Scale (Pinnell et al. 1995) and Zutell and Rasinski's (1991) Multidimensional Fluency Scale. For us, "attention to meaning" is paramount in assessing fluency, but we also want to examine readers' smoothness and pace and their impact on meaning making. Assessing the reading of narrative and expository text is particularly important when working with intermediate students. The form in Figure 6–1 can be used with any text and requires no special copying of text passages. It is meant to be used alongside a running record or informal reading inventory. It is easy to administer before, during, or at the end of a guided reading group (when other students in the group are otherwise occupied) or while conferring with students during independent reading. A valuable feature is the space for making notes about particular text challenges. These notes help

Student's name: _____ Date: _____

Title of text: _____ Level: _____ instructional _____ independent

Text type: _____ narrative _____ expository _____ other (note type) _____

Notes about text challenges/structures _____

Accuracy: _____ # of miscues, _____ # of self-corrections   Student's score (out of 12) _____

ATTENTION TO MEANING

4 — Reads in long, meaningful phrases that convey tone and structure of text. Chunking or phrasing is consistent with author's meaning and intent. The listener can understand content or narrative based on the student's interpretative reading. Although some deviations and/or repetitions may be present, reading is, for the most part, appropriately expressive and accurate. Miscues maintain meaning and reader self-corrects most errors. Consistent attention to text signals (punctuation, sentence boundaries, bold or italicized text).

3 — Reads in shorter phrases that mostly convey tone and structure of text. Chunking or phrasing may be choppy at times, although most of the reading is consistent with author's meaning and intent. Generally, the listener can understand content or narrative based on the student's reading even though little or no interpretation or expression is present. Fair accuracy. Miscues mostly consistent with meaning. Some self-corrections noted. Intermittent attention to text signals.

2 — Reads primarily in short, two- to three-word phrases with segments of word-by-word reading. Phrasing may be inappropriate, altering the author's meaning and intent. Sometimes difficult for the listener to understand content or narrative based on student's reading. If expression and intonation are present, they seem inappropriate and awkward. Frequent miscues that often alter meaning. Little or no attention to text signals.

1 — Reads mostly word by word with occasional chunks or phrases that may or may not be appropriate. Choppy, halting reading that limits and obscures meaning. Many miscues, few self-corrections.

SMOOTHNESS

4 — Overall, the reading sounds smooth, with appropriate breaks.

3 — Overall the reading sounds smooth, with occasional breaks that involve regressions, word-solving difficulties, and structural confusion from which reader recovers quickly.

2 — Overall the reading sounds choppy, with occasional smooth segments. There are many rough spots with numerous breaks, hesitations, and repetitions.

1 — Overall the reading is halting and choppy, with continual breaks, hesitations, and repetitions.

PACE   READING RATE (WPM): _____

4 — Appropriate to the text read.

3 — Uneven, but generally appropriate to text read.

2 — Slow, plodding, with a few appropriately paced segments.

1 — Very slow and laborious throughout.

FIG. 6–1 *Fluency Check (Teacher Version)*

you plan instruction that supports your students' reading of new and challenging expository text as well as complex or unfamiliar narratives.

When first using this form, it may help to record the reading, then analyze and score it while listening to the tape. Procedures for administering and scoring a fluency check are simple:

1. Select text the child can read with ninety to one hundred percent accuracy, ideally a text she is currently reading in another context.

2. Ask the child to read a section of text silently, then reread it orally. (For older students, this may be one or two pages; for younger readers, it may be an entire picture book.)

3. Rate the oral reading in each of the three areas.

4. Assign a composite score for the reading (from 3 to 12).

5. Confirm the score by asking the child to retell quickly what she remembers about the passage. How you approach this will vary with the type of comprehension skills you are stressing. Instead of retelling, you could ask a reader to:
   - Make a prediction about what will happen next.
   - Draw a conclusion about a character's motives, actions, or feelings.
   - Make an inference.

6. Note areas of concern.

7. Plan appropriate follow-up fluency teaching or coaching.

If a reader scores between 9 and 12, he is reading relatively fluently in that particular level and genre of text. Scores of 8 and below indicate that certain aspects of fluency are probably not in place for the reader at that particular level in that genre. However, the score a child receives is not nearly as valuable as the information gained about the areas where he possesses strengths or needs improvement.

If, after listening to a reader, you are concerned about peculiar or choppy phrasing, you might do a follow-up phrasing check. The following phrasing check is adapted from Rasinski's (2003) Phrased Text Lesson (140–42).

1. Select a passage at the student's instructional level. This could be a passage from something he is currently reading or a passage from an informal reading inventory.

2. Make a copy of the passage for both the student and yourself.

3. Ask the student to read the passage silently, then reread it orally.

4. As he reads orally, place slashes to indicate how he "chunks" the text.

5. Rate this information according to the criteria in "smoothness" section of the Fluency Check. See Figure 6–1.

You can also conduct a phrasing check/running record for a small group or the whole class during guided reading. The procedure is essentially the same:

1. Select and copy an entire text that the group will read silently.

2. As students read silently, circulate, signaling individual readers in turn to read aloud softly.

3. Mark each child's name in the text where he or she begins and ends.

4. Note miscues and phrasing on the copy of text.

Once you are familiar with fluency assessments, these procedures are easily incorporated into literacy routines because they *use materials children are already reading.*

Readers at all grade levels can reflect upon their reading (Opitz & Rasinski 1998; Rasinski 2003). They can also take responsibility for monitoring their own fluency by identifying their disfluent reading habits. The fluency check in Figure 6–2 has been adapted from a number of informal assessments we have used over the years including Opitz and Rasinski's (1998) Student Self-Evaluation (71). It is designed to be used by readers in grades 2 through 5, but it can be adapted to suit younger readers' developmental reading needs as well. Once students are familiar with how to use it, they can complete this fluency check every month or so, perhaps at a fluency center. Here's how it works:

1. The student selects a passage of one or two pages in a just-right book that she is able to read with ninety to one hundred percent accuracy.

2. The student first reads silently, then rereads orally using a tape recorder.

3. The student listens to the recording, then completes the fluency check form.

4. The teacher and the student discuss the assessment, what makes reading hard, and how to improve fluency.

▪ Assessment in Action

Remember Nick, Josh, and Carly, whom you met in Chapter 1? Let's complete a fluency check for each of them to get some practice in using the form.

Name: _____ Date: _____

Title of text:

_____

Text type: _____ fiction _____ nonfiction _____ other _____

Pages read: _____ My rating of book: _____ 4 _____ 3 _____ 2 _____ 1 _____ 0

                                                    Great   Good   Fair   Blah   Bad

1. I remember what I read and can tell about it.   _____   _____   _____   _____

                                           Yes   Some   Not much   No

2. I read smoothly.   _____   _____   _____   _____

                    Yes   Pretty smooth   A little choppy   Really choppy

3. I read so that others can understand.   _____   _____   _____   _____

                                Yes   Mostly   A little   Not much

4. I _____ recommend _____ don't recommend this book because _____

_____

5. Tricky parts of this book were _____

_____

6. Other responses I have to the book (drawings or writing)

FIG. 6–2 *Fluency Check (Student Version)*

Nick

Nick's pace and smoothness are strong, earning him 3s in each of these categories. But he struggles to access and use information. There is little expressiveness
to his reading, and he is not particularly attentive to text signals. His reading
conveys little sense of content, substance, or tone. So his attention-to-meaning
rating is somewhere between 2 and 3. When we question him about what he

has read, the depth of his lack of comprehension becomes apparent. His overall score, then, is between 8 and 9, but as an older reader his disfluency, which may well be the cause of his lack of comprehension, has a negative impact upon his achievement.

Josh

Josh's strange, inappropriate expression merits a score of 2 in all three areas, for an overall score of 6. This is well below what would be considered fluent. His reading rate, although not unusually slow, is not what it should be, given Josh's strong word-solving skills. Despite his disfluent behavior, Josh does retain some sense of story if he is questioned after reading short segments of text or given a question in advance. With fluency coaching, all areas of Josh's reading should become smoother and stronger. He possesses strengths—a keen interest in nature and wide and varied knowledge of animals and the natural world—that will work more reliably for him once fluency issues are resolved.

Carly

A beginning reader who is still putting skills and strategies together, Carly does not yet move flexibly between cueing systems. Although she reads text at her instructional level with ninety percent accuracy, she tends to overrely on the visual aspects. (This is not uncommon for a reader at her stage of development.) Even when weaned from using her finger as a tracking device, she still reads haltingly, in short two- or three-word phrases or chunks, with little expression. Sometimes the chunking makes sense semantically, other times it does not. She stops often to reread and study text and pictures. Carly scores a 2 on attention to meaning and smoothness. Her pace is slow and plodding, but better without her finger—uneven, but generally appropriate to the text she is reading. Here she gets a score of 3.

■ From Assessment to Instruction

There is no "one-size-fits-all" coaching or instruction that applies to every child. You need to focus on different areas of fluency with different children. To select a fluency technique that best suits an individual student or small groups of students, consider the following questions.

- Does the student read word by word all of the time?

- Does the student read word by word frequently, yet manage to read some phrases more fluently?

- Does the student not recognize enough words to read fluently?

- Does the student read too slowly?

- Does the student attempt to sound out unknown words?

- Does the student appear to be using meaning as she attempts to decode unknown words?

- Does the student use correct syntax (language structure) when "guessing" at unknown words?

- Does the student seem to recall details but not interpretive concepts?

- Does the student show confidence when reading to you? Is he willing to take a risk with unknown words?

- Is the student comfortable reading to a partner?

- Does the student have the confidence to read orally in front of peers?

- What, if any, expression does the child use?

- Does the child's intonation and expression convey meaning?

- Where does the student fit on the fluency rubric?

- Is the student's reading rate near grade-level expectations?

- What are your goals for this student?

How each question is answered helps determine which strategies best suit each student. Figure 6–3, Strategies for Fluency, matches strategies with traits of disfluent readers. To use the chart, identify the perceived problem or problems, then select strategies that target those fluency needs.

■ Instruction in Action

Based on the assessments of Nick, Josh, and Carly, what kinds of specific instruction will help them become better, more fluent readers?

STRATEGIES	ASPECTS OF FLUENCY FOR DEVELOPMENT												
	Confidence	Word Recognition (Minimal)	Word Recognition (Moderate)	Attempting Unknown Words	Expression	Engagement	Rate	Comprehension	Inferencing	Motivation	Processing	Tone	Phrasing
Collaborative Reading (Ch. 7)	X		X		X	X	X	X		X	X	X	
Shared Reading (Ch. 8)	X	X			X	X	X	X	X	X	X	X	X
Choral Reading (Ch. 9)	X				X	X	X	X		X	X	X	X
Echo Reading (Ch. 10)	X	X	X	X	X	X	X					X	X
Fluency Flexors (Ch. 11)	X	X		X	X	X	X	X	X	X	X	X	X
Radio Reading (Ch. 12)			X		X	X	X		X	X		X	
Getting into Character (Ch. 13)	X		X		X	X	X	X	X	X	X	X	X
Poetry (Ch. 14)	X	X			X		X	X	X	X	X	X	X
Readers Theatre (Ch. 15)	X	X			X	X	X	X	X	X	X	X	X
Plays (Ch. 16)	X		X		X			X	X			X	X
Environmental Print (Ch. 17)		X					X	X	X				X
Repeated Readings (Ch. 18)	X		X	X	X		X	X					X
Text Signals (Ch. 19)					X	X	X		X			X	X
Writing (Ch. 20)		X	X	X		X	X	X			X	X	X
Humorous Text (Ch. 21)	X		X			X	X		X			X	X
Series Books (Ch. 22)			X		X	X	X	X	X	X	X	X	X
Sorting Words (Ch. 23)		X	X	X		X	X				X		
Chunking Words (Ch. 24)	X	X		X							X		
Chunking Phrases (Ch. 25)	X		X	X	X	X					X		

FIG. 6–3 *Strategies for Fluency*

Nick

Although Nick's reading is fast and accurate, he reads with little expression and almost no attention to meaning. As a third grader with strong visual and auditory skills, Nick has spent a number of years developing his reading style. One or two quick fluency lessons will probably not change the habits he has come to rely on—it is very hard for learners to relinquish behavior that has brought them confidence and respect as readers. Nick's explicit fluency instruction must therefore be ongoing, as integral to the literacy program as attention to word solving, comprehension, and vocabulary.

Activities such as "say it like the character" from Opitz and Rasinski's *Goodbye Round Robin* and "interpreted rereadings" will focus his attention on intonation, inflection, and meaning. He will also benefit from exposure to many genres. Here are a few additional ideas:

● Fluency flexors (Chapter 11) will support his rereading of text "as the author intended."

● Expressive reading of poetry (Chapter 14) and plays (Chapter 16) will encourage him to read with feeling and intonation.

● Readers theatre (Chapter 15) will take advantage of his reading accuracy, enabling him to focus on performing with peers.

● Reading to younger students will also capitalize on his strengths while helping him attend to expression, intonation, and active engagement with text. In preparing, he will practice reading expressively, using different voices for characters and attending to text features such as bold or italicized print.

Josh

Josh has worked hard to perfect his singsong style designed to "make reading more exciting." He will benefit from models of fluent reading such as teacher read-alouds and opportunities to read with peers as partners. He will also benefit from specific attention to smooth, fluent reading by way of a variety of guided oral rereading strategies. A few additional ideas for Josh include:

● Listening to himself on tape, then rereading, will give him the opportunity to compare his reading to the models he hears daily during teacher read-aloud and shared reading (Chapter 8). He can then learn to "fix up" his reading independently.

- Echo reading (Chapter 10), radio reading (Chapter 12), and choral reading (Chapter 9) will all provide modeling, guided practice, and time for independent performance.

- Chunking phrases (Chapter 25) through games and rereading will help him smooth out the reading process. The sentences and phrases of fluency flexors (Chapter 11) extend this chunking into longer text, moving him closer to appropriately expressive reading.

- Plays (Chapter 16), poetry (Chapter 14), and getting-into-character activities (Chapter 13) will provide opportunities to read and reread text meant to be practiced and read aloud. Such practice is valuable in weaning him from his inefficient attention to reading word by word.

- Readers theatre (Chapter 15) is an alternative way to "make reading exciting" while enhancing his fluent, confident reading of text.

- Creating and reading humorous texts (Chapter 21) is an exciting alternative reading-and-writing activity for building his fluency.

Carly

The youngest of the three readers described in Chapter 1, Carly's disfluent habits have just begun to develop. Her finger, an important tool as her reading abilities emerged, now slows her down. As she learns to give up the finger as a place-keeping tool, she needs fluency lessons that will help her grow into a smooth, capable reader. Certainly Carly, like all beginning readers, needs many models of fluent reading every day through teacher read-alouds, shared reading (Chapter 8), and choral reading (Chapter 9). A few other strategies to support Carly's fluency are:

- Echo reading (Chapter 10) and collaborative reading (Chapter 7) with parents or older reading partners will offer her continuous models of fluent reading while at the same time providing additional eyes-on-text time.

- Fluency flexors (Chapter 11) will give her opportunities to reread, rehearse, and share familiar sentences and short paragraphs, and experience the feel and sound of fluency.

- Poetry (Chapter 14), plays (Chapter 16), readers theatre (Chapter 15), and getting-into-character activities (Chapter 13) will give her engaging opportunities to read text meant to be read aloud, help her reach higher, and enhance her fluency, confidence, and motivation in more complex and challenging texts.

Collaborating Strategies

Collaborative Reading

7

■ What Is It, Why Use It?

In collaborative reading, two or more readers, together, process text accurately and fluently. Collaborative reading provides peer-to-peer accountability in a social context, allowing students to build literacy skills, strategies, and knowledge as they put their heads together over text. It gives them more practice and experience with text, which is essential in building fluency, confidence, and flexibility in applying reading skills. Having a partner helps young readers read longer (Griffin 2000, 2002). Reading with a peer or older reader also promotes more fluent, expressive reading. Collaborative reading takes many forms; in a sense, most of the strategies in this book involve some sort of collaboration.

■ Using It in the Classroom

Collaborative reading strategies aimed at improving fluency primarily involve two readers sitting side by side, reading text orally. (There are also many excellent models of collaborative silent reading, but they are not our focus here.) Many classrooms have a "buddy reading" center. In others, partner reading is a choice students make after completing center activities or other independent work.

Peer Partnerships in a Nutshell

In a peer partnership, two readers of approximately equal ability construct the meaning of a text together. This strategy is most appropriate for beginning or emergent readers, but if the focus is on rereading for expression, it also supports older readers' fluency.

Research has demonstrated that with a strategizing partner at their side, young readers read longer, strengthen their fluency, jointly construct meaning, and solve words together (Griffin 2000; MacGillivray 1997; MacGillivray & Hawes 1994; Rhodes & Shanklin 1993). Although peer partners are not completely independent, these relationships provide important bridges between dependency on the teacher and solo reading.

In collaborative peer partnerships, young readers decide what works best for them, individually and together. Let's observe a peer partnership in action. Emergent readers Kitty and Bobby sit side by side at a table, a copy of *Spider,*

FIG. 7–1 *Buddy Reading*

Spider (Cowley 1987) open between them. On page 2, Kitty points to the first word as Bobby reads, *Bee, bee, come to tea.* Kitty then repeats, *Bee, bee, come to tea,* and says, "How 'bout if you say it first, then I'll say it," effectively negotiating a turn-taking structure that works for her.

Here are the procedural steps:

1. Pair students of approximately equal reading ability as assessed by a running record, miscue analysis, and/or other tools.

2. The partners select a book and a comfortable reading spot, sitting side by side.

3. Partners either take turns reading alternate pages or read in unison.

4. Partners return to the whole group to share strategies and discoveries. (Strategies may also be discussed before partner reading. Either way these discussions are an essential means of highlighting and supporting effective collaborative behavior.)

5. (Optional) Partners write and/or draw about their collaboration. This helps readers think about and internalize what works.

You need to pair students to best meet each individual reader's social, emotional, and academic needs. We pair students who we believe will work well together and keep the partnerships in effect for four to six weeks, allowing time in which to build a supportive, collaborative reading relationship.

The books readers choose can come from many sources: leveled-book browsing boxes, just-right books in the classroom library, books previously read during guided reading or other instructional contexts. Familiar or favorite texts are excellent choices for peer partners, because they are freed from the problem solving required in a first or second reading and can attend to fluency, expression, and interpretation. With a peer at their side, readers play with familiar text, chanting it, singing it, shouting it, and otherwise making it their own. They also engage in text-related discussion that deepens understanding. Joy Richardson says, "Because they reread the books so many times, they notice things. They make connections to characters and connections between stories, themes, ideas, and characters. They also ask better questions about the books because they really know them."

Some teachers provide book bags, folders, or baskets in which students store their partner reading books. You may also ask partners to keep brief records of their work together. Writing about what they think and feel when they read together also helps partners focus on the strategies being encouraged. Students can

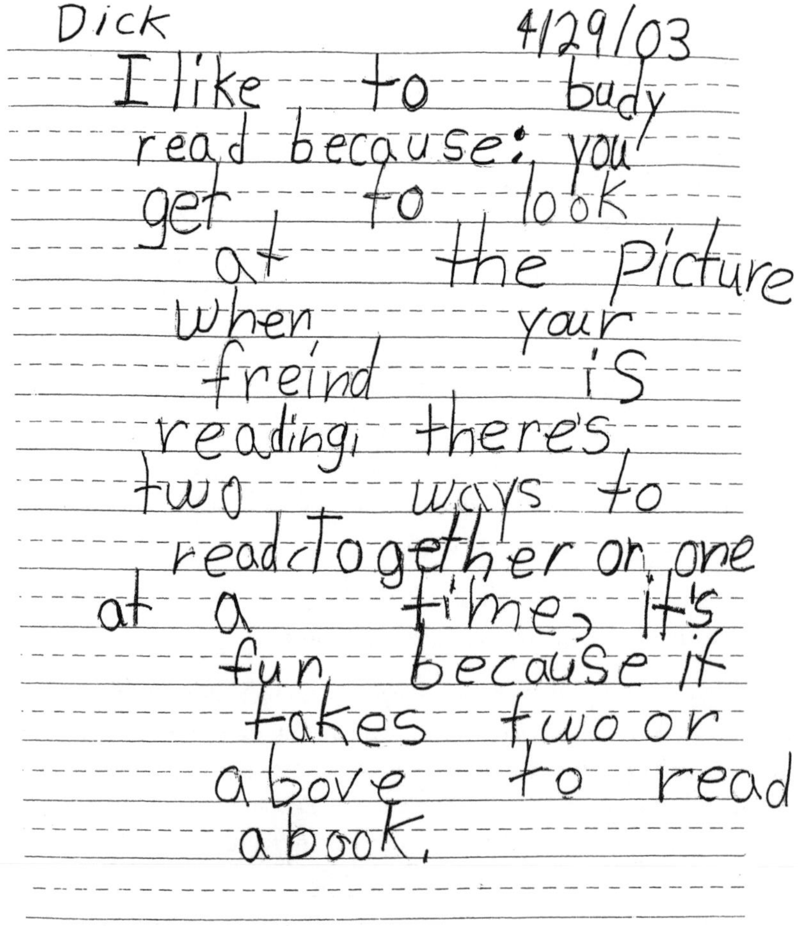

Dick   4/29/03
I like to buddy
read because: you
get to look
at the picture
when your
freind is
reading; there's
two ways to
read together or one
at a time, it's
fun because it
takes two or
above to read
a book.

FIG. 7-2 *"Buddy Reading," Writing Sample*

read these responses aloud during group sharing, a very personalized kind of fluency practice. A resource in planning, implementing, and supporting peer partnerships is *Shoulder to Shoulder: Moving Toward Independence Through Peer Partnerships* (Prescott-Griffin 2005).

Cross-Ability Paired Reading in a Nutshell

Cross-ability paired reading (Samway, Whang, & Pippitt 1995; Muldowney 1995; Nes 1997; Topping & Lindsay 1992) is appropriate for readers in grades

K–5. In cross-ability partnerships, a more capable reader (tutor) supports the efforts of a younger, less mature reader (tutee). As developed by Keith Topping (1987, 1989), it was originally designed for parents and children, but it can also be used effectively in the classroom. Possible pairings include:

- Teacher and student

- Classroom aide or volunteer and student

- Student and student

The steps are these:

1. The tutee selects reading material at her instructional level. Tutors may suggest texts, but the tutee should be allowed to choose texts that interest her.

2. Paired readers then find a comfortable reading spot.

3. Before reading, tutor and tutee establish silent signals to indicate when the tutee wants to read by herself or is tired and needs a break. (In the latter case, the tutor takes over, reading alone for a short time until the tutee once again joins in.)

4. Readers begin reading in unison.

5. If the tutee miscues, then corrects the word, the tutor offers praise. Five seconds after an uncorrected miscue the tutor tells the word. (Student-to-student cross-ability paired readers can be told to count to five before supplying the word.) After the tutee says the correct word, unison reading continues.

6. At some point the tutee should signal that she wants to read solo.

7. At the end of a session, tutor and tutee talk about how the reading went. The tutor praises the tutee's efforts and indicates areas where she can improve.

8. The pair might also discuss difficult words or interesting ideas in the text, centering their thoughts on meaning.

9. Paired readers might also complete a paired reading log (see Appendix A) or response form (see Appendix B). Both the log and the response form have been adapted from the work of Rasinski (2003). They provide information about paired-reading sessions, but the response form is particularly helpful in focusing readers' attention on fluency and the progress they are making.

Topping (1989) suggests that cross-ability paired reading take place at least three times a week for a minimum of six weeks, each session lasting approximately fifteen to thirty minutes.

When pairing students, it's generally best to pair older and younger students from different classrooms and grade levels. These groupings benefit both tutor and tutee. In fact, some research suggests that the older students derive the most benefit from such experiences (Topping 1989). Nevertheless, if the focus is on practicing already familiar text, the readers can be students in the same classroom at different ability levels. The more experienced peer coaches the rereading in preparation for a performance for the whole class.

No matter how readers are paired, training the tutor will ensure that the model is used effectively to support readers in decoding text too difficult for them to read independently. The video, *Using Paired Reading to Help Your Students Become Better Readers, Grades 1–6* (Burrill & Paulson 1998) provides clear, specific training for paired-reading tutors.

■ Connecting It to Independent Reading

Deliberately focusing on fluency, word identification, and comprehension during and after paired reading supports reader thinking on many levels. Our goal is for students at all stages of development to carry the strategies practiced during collaborative reading with them into their independent reading. Paired-reading tutors, who know the tutees' strengths, weaknesses, and interests, can also help them select just-right books, both for the collaborative reading sessions and for independent reading. In some schools, when paired reading was used regularly over at least four to six weeks, students made significant gains in reading development (Topping 1989).

■ Bringing It Home

Because peer partnerships involve readers of approximately equal expertise, this model is most appropriate in primary classrooms with beginning readers. However, cross-ability paired reading was originally designed for parents and children and is therefore an ideal strategy to "bring home." Paired reading is a supportive way in which family members and caregivers can strengthen children's literacy skills.

Training is essential and can best be accomplished through a meeting during which you demonstrate the process or show a video like *Using Paired Reading.* In lieu of such training, you must at the very least send home clear and explicit directions for parents about how to pair-read with their children (see Appendix C). Paired reading logs and response sheets can be included, with a request that children return them to school when completed.

▪ Using It with English Language Learners

As young children learn to speak and read in a second language, talk and interaction are critical. English language learners need many, varied opportunities to engage in real reading and writing. Authentic literacy activities like peer reading partnerships and cross-ability paired reading support all children, but especially English language learners. Although talk about books and strategies benefits all young readers, it is especially important for children struggling to master a new language. Giving book talks on independent reading titles introduces language and conceptual terms to students as well as linking concepts to illustrations in the text.

Many schools have volunteer reading programs in which community members regularly read aloud to children, usually during lunch once or twice a week. Often these programs target English language learners or those whose language background is restricted in some other way. These extra reading aloud times provide young readers with fluent models of reading written text while building their conceptual knowledge, vocabulary, and comprehension. Such reading programs are ideal venues for cross-ability paired reading. Once trained, reading volunteers can alternate between reading aloud to and reading along with students.

Props also help readers become more engaged in the reading process. This engagement is especially important for English language learners. Props support readers' participation in reading and in postreading activities like retelling. Simple props might be puppets (or masks made from paper plates) depicting the characters in the story. Authors like Jan Brett (www.janbrett.com) have websites with templates for masks, puppets, and other props based on their stories.

▪ What to Read

Any kind of text can be used for peer reading partnerships and cross-ability paired reading. In both cases, the material should be interesting to the readers and should lend itself to reading aloud. Peer partners often select familiar texts to reread and practice. They might also select more challenging text at their instructional level, putting their heads together to construct meaning together.

Traditionally, texts for cross-ability paired reading are at the tutee's instructional level, texts that offer some challenges but that can be handled with support. Cross-ability pairs can also reread familiar texts at the tutee's independent reading level, the tutor coaching for fluent, expressive reading in performance.

Primary Titles

Wacky Wednesday (LeSieg 1974)

You Read to Me, I'll Read to You: Very Short Stories to Read Together (Hoberman 2001)

Intermediate Titles

I Am Phoenix: Poems for Two Voices (Fleischman 1986)

Joyful Noise: Poems for Two Voices (Fleischman 1988)

Should There Be Zoos? A Persuasive Text (Stead 2000)

Shared Reading

8

What Is It, Why Use It?

Shared reading is based on Don Holdaway's (1979) idea of "shared book experiences." During shared reading, you model fluent, expressive reading by sharing big books, picture books, chart-size poems and stories, or other large-print text with students either as a class or in small groups. Books may be (but don't always have to be) above readers' independent or instructional reading levels, thus encouraging them to read "a head taller" with the support of modeling and repeated practice. During shared reading you model your enjoyment of reading as well as how you think about and use reading strategies. With younger students, the text is often a big book; hold up the book and point as you read, calling children's attention to concepts about print such as:

- Left-to-right processing

- Word-by-word matching

- Letters, words, sentences

- First, last, next

- Text signals: punctuation (periods, commas, question marks, quotation marks, exclamation marks), bold or italicized print, capital letters

- Sound, letter, and word patterns

- Rhyming words

FIG. 8–1 *Shared Reading Lesson*

Shared reading builds listeners' language skills and vocabulary, establishing patterns and habits that promote lifelong reading. By listening to expert modeling, listeners internalize rhythms and patterns of written English and become familiar with narrative themes and expository text structures. Shared reading also allows listeners to explore feelings, situations, and problems that go beyond their own experience. As they live vicariously through the stories and characters, listeners compare and contrast their own experiences with the experiences of others.

■ Using It in the Classroom

Shared reading is a way to introduce listeners to many models of continuous text. The procedures are simple and can be adapted to any grade level, K–5. You must decide what works best for your students.

Shared Reading in a Nutshell

1. Select interesting text.
2. Introduce the text, possibly discussing illustrations and asking students to make predictions.

3. Read the text with expression, intonation, and appropriate pacing. (With primary students, point to words and pause often, asking the students to supply predictable or repeated words or phrases.)

4. Pause as necessary during reading to:
   - Discuss text features.
   - Ask students for predictions or conclusions.
   - Ask students to make a connection to their own experience or another text.

5. After reading, you may reread the whole text or segments of text while discussing text features or content. You may also ask literal and inferential questions about characters, plot, and setting.

6. Encourage students to respond:
   - During whole-group discussion
   - During small-group discussion
   - During partner discussion
   - In writing

Variations and Applications

Varieties of shared reading are numerous, depending on the age of the students, the texts selected, and curricular needs. Here are just a few:

- *Reading along.* As you read, invite students to read along during familiar portions of the text (repeated phrases or sentences, predictable rhymes, choruses).

- *Echoing.* Read a line or two and have your students echo you. (For more information on echo reading, see Chapter 10.)

- *Reading fast or reading slow.* Read text fast or slow as appropriate. Following the reading, ask students questions like:
  - How did my reading sound?
  - What did you notice?
  - Why do you think I read the way I did?
  - What did you notice about the words?

■ Connecting It to Independent Reading

As children reread these now-familiar shared texts and then go on to read new texts they've chosen, they are more likely to apply and practice strategies learned during shared reading.

■ Bringing It Home

One of the most important literacy practices in the home is reading aloud. Parent and child, side by side, reading a book the child has chosen is the best and most personalized kind of shared reading. Encourage parents and caregivers to follow shared reading procedures such as pointing to words as they read, pausing to let their child read a predictable word or phrase, and discussing with their child what she or he has noticed about text, content, and story. We suggest that parents read aloud in books just slightly above children's reading level. (Appendix D is a sample letter for this purpose.) When families ask for read-aloud ideas, send home a list of your class' favorite books and encourage them to visit public libraries and local bookstores and select books that they love and that interest their children.

■ Using It with English Language Learners

English language learners need many opportunities to hear fluent reading of a wide variety of texts. They also need to be able to follow along visually in order to increase the number of words they recognize, their vocabulary, and their sense of story and textual structures. English language conventions such as punctuation, grammar, and syntax are often very different from an English language learner's first language. Shared reading provides opportunities to hear about and discuss English language conventions and structures. "Following along" with fluent readers by supplying a word or phrase gives English language learners a means of participating without the pressure of performing (Tompkins 2004). Because shared reading of stories and nonfiction texts is such a valuable strategy for English language learners, you may want to arrange additional opportunities for them to hear books read aloud:

- Invite volunteers from the community to come regularly to read to a student or students during lunch or another free period.

- Form partnerships between your students and students in other grades.

- Encourage them to participate in public library read-aloud programs.

■ What to Read

Text for shared reading should first and foremost be interesting and engaging, lending itself to repeated readings. Text needs to be visually accessible to readers through big books, charts, or overhead projectors, so that they can focus their attention on the words as you model. Alphabet books, of which there are hundreds, also make great shared reading texts. Older students can read along silently in individual copies of the shared text as you read aloud.

Primary Titles

Don't Step on the Crack! (McNaughton 2000)

Koala Lou (Fox 1988)

Joseph Had a Little Overcoat (Taback 1999)

Let's Go Visiting (Williams 2003)

Mrs. Wishy Washy (Cowley 1989), and others in this series

No, David (Shannon 1998), and other books in this series

Panda Bear, Panda Bear, What Do You See? (Martin & Archambault 2003)

Rub-a-Dub Sub (Ashman 2003)

Someday (Zolotow 1965)

Suddenly! (McNaughton 1994)

Thomas Knew There Were Pirates in the Bathroom (Parker 1990)

Top Cat (Ehlert 1998)

We're Going on a Bear Hunt (Rosen & Oxenbury 1989)

Who's in the Shed? (Parkes 1986)

Wilfred Gordon McDonald Partridge (Fox 1985)

Alphabet Books

A Is for Salad (Lester 2000)

Alaska A B C Book (Kreeger & Cartwright 1978)

Into the A, B, Sea (Rose 2000)

K Is for Kissing a Cool Kangaroo (Andrzae & Rees 2002)

Sharkabet: A Sea of Sharks from A to Z (Troll 2002)

Tomorrow's Alphabet (Shannon 1996)

Intermediate Titles

Shared reading with intermediate students is best done using texts they are reading in other contexts or poems, plays, and lyrical verse meant to be read aloud. Specific choices depend on reader interest and your curricular goals.

Choral Reading

9

■ What Is It, Why Use It?

Choral reading, or reading in unison (Gillett & Temple 2000), increases children's awareness of the rhythms, conventions, and structures of written language as they work together to "perform" text. Worthy and Broaddus (2002) write that "fluency gives language its musical quality, its rhythm and flow, and makes reading sound effortless" (334). As a teacher you want children to feel the rhythm and flow of written language, to appreciate its musical qualities, and to internalize this understanding as they read aloud and silently. You also want students to understand the many ways that sentence structure and punctuation signify meaning. When students read chorally, all these aspects of fluent, successful reading come together in a supportive, nurturing context.

Reading chorally also increases reading rate. In concert with others, children experience the joy and satisfaction of fluent, successful reading, increasing their eyes-on-text time. Choral reading strengthens readers' word recognition and vocabulary skills while enabling them to *feel* what it means to be fluent.

■ Using It in the Classroom

Choral reading is a strategy that can be used in whole or small groups, or when children read as partners. Procedures are simple and easily adapted to any text. For example, Jenny Baumeister and her students have just shared in writing a story entitled "Facts About Camels." As Jenny points to the text written on chart paper, children reread the story in unison with appropriate expository emphasis and expression.

Choral Reading in a Nutshell

1. Select a short text to read aloud. The text must be visible to all students—a big book, a chart, or individual copies. For younger readers large-print text works best, focusing everyone's attention in one place.

2. Read with expression, taking time to discuss aspects of the text such as content, illustrations, and concepts about print. You may then reread the text a second or third time, depending on its difficulty and your readers' need for more practice.

3. Invite your students to reread the text with you.

4. Read the text chorally with your students one or more times.

5. Have the students read the text chorally without you.

Variations and Applications

There are many variations and applications of choral reading, depending on the age of your students, their reading preferences, the texts you use, and your curriculum. As a primary-grade teacher, Mary Lee used choral reading regularly to read and practice new "shared texts" (more challenging texts that she and the class read and reread together many times). Typically, after a group choral reading, primary graders "partner up" and chorally reread the text a third time to practice fluency before completing a reader-response activity. Teachers of older students often use choral reading to introduce and practice poetry, plays, and other interpretive readings. Asking students to read chorally, even once a week, gives them regular opportunities to participate in fluent, expressive performance of text. Here are a few suggestions for using and extending choral reading:

- *Reading along with tapes.* Individually or in small groups, readers listen and read along with recordings of text read at a pace appropriate for them. Marie Carbo's recorded books (*www.nrsi.com*) and Living Books (*www.livingbooks.com*), a computer program, are two sources of such recordings.

- *Echoing.* Divide the class or group into two parts and have them echo each other. Half the group reads a sentence, paragraph, or page chorally, then the other half echoes the same sentence, paragraph, or page.

- *Reading and singing songs.* The group reads or sings the verses of songs written on chart paper, on handouts, or in individual songbooks.

- *Conducting.* Choosing a "conductor," or leader, helps maintain the pace of the choral reading, especially if the teacher is not reading along. The conductor holds a "baton" (rulers, chopsticks, and short pointers work well) and reads in a slightly louder voice, the "orchestra" following her lead. Children love acting as the conductor and in doing so, they focus on the beat, rhythm, and style of a particular piece of writing.

- *Reading poems by stanzas.* After reading a poem together, divide the poem into stanzas and have small groups or pairs of students each practice a stanza. Then reread the poem, with each subgroup performing their assigned stanza.

- *Assigning dialogue and narration.* When a story has a lot of dialogue, have one subgroup read the narration and as many subgroups as there are characters read the appropriate dialogue. Short, amusing texts like Lobel's *Fables* (1980) work especially well.

■ Connecting It to Independent Reading

Rehearsal is a critical aspect of choral reading. If you ask readers of any age to read chorally, you should first give them the opportunity to practice individually, either orally or silently. Then they can gather as a group to reread and practice together. In "almost independent" contexts like pairs and groups of three or four, students often support one another's performance. Choral reading smooths out readers' pacing, expression, and comprehension, deepening an individual's engagement when he reads alone.

Choral reading is a supportive center activity for two readers or a small group. Choral reading could take place at a fluency center, reading center, or listening center. In the latter case, children read along with tapes. Protocols for choral reading as a center activity might include:

- How to read in a soft ("inside," "five-inch") voice

- How to allocate portions of text

- How to monitor and respect appropriate pacing

■ Bringing It Home

Choral reading is a flexible reading strategy for caregivers and children. They can read newspapers, magazines, books—any print materials they choose. It is a powerful way to model literacy and reinforce the benefits of practice. Choral reading is also an integral part of paired reading (Topping 1987, 1989), a strategy developed especially for use by family members and children. (For more on paired reading, see Chapter 7.)

▪ Using It with English Language Learners

Choral reading allows English language learners to join in fluent reading of text without the pressure of solo performance. As they listen to and practice with classmates, they learn English pronunciation, vocabulary, sentence patterns, and conventions. As a prereading activity before whole-group choral reading, you could pair English language learners with fluent readers who have already practiced the selection. You might also meet with small groups to preview a text, reading and rereading it to them *before* introducing to the whole group:

- Use illustrations to talk students through the text.

- Introduce words, concepts, and important text signals readers should look for when reading a second or third time or on their own.

- Read and reread text several times with exaggerated expression, inviting children to echo you in places.

Previewing helps all learners come to a whole-group choral reading with the linguistic tools and background to keep up and enjoy reading in unison.

▪ What to Read

Any text can be used successfully for choral reading as long as it is interesting and not too difficult. Try to choose choral reading texts that are at or just slightly above your students' instructional reading level. Lyrical, rhyming texts make ideal choices, but the sky's the limit.

Primary Titles

Brown Bear, Brown Bear, What Do You See? (Martin 1983)

Chicka Chicka Boom Boom (Martin & Archambault 1989)

Chicken Soup with Rice (Sendak 1987)

Chickens Aren't the Only Ones (Heller 1981), or any book by Ruth Heller

A House Is a House for Me (Hoberman 1978)

You Read to Me, I'll Read to You: Very Short Stories to Read Together (Hoberman 2001)

In the Night Kitchen (Sendak 1970)

"Slowly, Slowly, Slowly," Said the Sloth (Carle 2002)

Intermediate Titles

Bringing the Rain to Kapiti Plain (Aardema 1981)

I Am Phoenix: Poems for Two Voices (Fleischman 1986)

A Joyful Noise: Poems for Two Voices (Fleischman 1988)

Singable Books

Down by the Bay (Westcott 1998a)

Five Little Ducks (Aruego & Dewey 1986)

Here We Go Round the Mulberry Bush (Hillenbrand 2003)

I Know an Old Lady Who Swallowed a Fly (Westcott 2003)

The Lady with the Alligator Purse (Westcott 1988b)

Old MacDonald Had a Farm (Alley 1991)

Seals on the Bus (Hart 2000)

Sitting Down to Eat (Harley 1996)

Skip to My Lou (Westcott 1988c)

Wheels on the Bus (Wickstrom 1985)

Take Me Out of the Bathtub and Other Silly Dilly Songs (Katz 2001)

This Little Light of Mine (Lisberg 2003)

10 Purposeful Oral Reading

■ What Is It, Why Use It?

Purposeful oral reading with varieties like echo reading, neurological impress, purposeful oral rereading, and call and response allows you to support beginning readers by modeling strong, expressive reading. It fosters the ability to recognize words independently and read in a smooth, expressive style. It allows students to read orally without fear of embarrassment or ridicule.

■ Using It in the Classroom

Purposeful oral reading can be done with small groups or the whole class. First the students follow along silently while you read aloud; then they read the same passage aloud themselves. In this way, they get to hear the correct pronunciation and expression just before they have to read it themselves.

Echo Reading in a Nutshell

Echo reading (Cecil 2003; Johns & Lenski 1997; Rasinski 2003) is just what the name implies. Holding the text in the students' view, you read a sentence or phrase fluently, using correct tone, expression, and phrasing. The students then "echo" you by reading the same line. Some students benefit if you point to each word as you read and as they read.

1. Make sure the text is visible to all students. (If necessary, give students their own copy of the text.)

2. Point to each word and read orally while the children read silently.

3. Discuss the text and its meaning.

4. Return the pointer to the beginning of the line, and point to each word as the class "echos" the reading. Chime in if the readers seem to be struggling.

5. Repeat this process line by line until the whole text has been read.

6. Talk about the expression and intonation in the reading—the rhythm of *Brown Bear, Brown Bear, What Do You See?* (Martin 1983), for example, and the inflection used when asking a question.

7. Reread the whole text using the echoing procedure.

8. Visit this text often in the next few days, having students echo your reading each time.

Make certain students understand the word *echo*. Then practice "echoing" as a game, having students repeat short phrases ("We are great readers!" "We are a super class." "We love ice cream cones covered with olives.") Students will catch on quickly. Echo reading is best with short texts. Use a chart, big book, or a projected transparency so the text can be seen clearly by all students. Initially, it is best to start off with a short poem or rhyme, such as "One, Two, Buckle My Shoe."

Neurological Impress in a Nutshell (adapted from Johns & Lenski 1997)

Neurological impress (Heckelman 1966; Lipson & Wixson 1991) requires a one-on-one minitutorial. You stand or sit close behind the student, your mouth near the student's ear, as you read a short piece of text aloud together. The close proximity of your voice allows the student to hear a word instantaneously.

Neurological impress offers great support; it enables the reader to hear the correct words and expression at the same time they are reading the material. It also is very motivating, because the student does it with an adult. Following are the steps:

1. Select a text at the student's instructional level. (The text should be short; this minitutorial should last no more than three minutes.)

2. Sit slightly behind the student with your mouth close to the student's ear.

3. Explain to the student that this is a choral reading and that he must concentrate on saying the words along with you accurately and with expression.

4. If necessary, keep your finger under the words you are reading together.

5. Read slowly enough for the student to follow along, yet fast enough that there is a small challenge in keeping up.

6. Repeat the reading, and discuss any confusing parts. If there is a problem area, echo-read that section.

7. Explain that you will read this same text again together tomorrow but that in the meantime he can practice on his own.

8. As the student becomes more fluent with the text, speed up the reading.

9. Once the student is proficient and comfortable with a text, begin this process again with a new piece, perhaps in a different genre.

Purposeful Oral Rereading in a Nutshell

Many children love to read aloud, but are uncomfortable with round-robin or "popcorn" reading, which doesn't give them time to rehearse. *Purposeful* oral rereading is rereading for a reason:

- Read your favorite part.

- Read the part of the text that supports your answer.

- Read the part that made you decide such-and-such.

- Read the part in which you can tell that the character is beginning to change.

- Read a sentence that contains signal words.

- Read the section that sums up the main idea.

- Read the area you found confusing.

Call and Response in a Nutshell

Call and response is a type of singing in which the lead singer "calls" a line and the audience or chorus responds with a refrain. Call and response reading is similar. The response is one or two repetitive phrases that are read after the leader reads. You can find call and response texts on the web, or the class can write their own. Here's an example:

Call: Cinderella was a sweet young gal.

Response: Oh, yes, Cinderella was a sweet young gal.

Call: Cinderella had to clean the house and the cinders.

Response: Oh, yes, Cinderella was a sweet young gal.

Call: Cinderella did her sisters' hair for the ball.

Response: Oh, yes, Cinderella was a sweet young gal.

▧ Connecting It to Independent Reading

Anything read in class—books, charts, poems, magazines, whatever—should be available to be reread during independent reading. Children should be encouraged to "visit again" the materials they have enjoyed earlier. Mentioning some of the materials just before independent reading reminds students of what is available.

▧ Bringing It Home

Taking home a text that has been used for purposeful oral reading and sharing it with family members is excellent reinforcement. After a child is fluent with a text, she can bring the book home and read it to five different people, who then sign off on a slip of paper (see Appendix E, Listen to Me Read!). (Be sure to allow proxy signatures for distant relatives.)

▧ Using It with English Language Learners

English language learners may be able to decode words but not understand what they are reading. Or their cultural background may cause them to attribute a different meaning to certain words and phrases (Freeman & Freeman 2000).

Expression and pacing are extremely important for English language learners. You control the pacing of these strategies. Be sure to allow English language learners the time they need in order to be able to join in. Read slowly enough to give English language learners time to receive the message but fast enough to help them gain fluency.

■ What to Read

Books with repetitive passages work well for purposeful oral reading. (Texts that rhyme give students hints of the pattern to come.) For a neurological impress it is best if the pictures and text give clues to the meaning of the words (books using rebuses, for example).

Primary Titles

Piggies (Wood & Wood 1999)

Why a Dog? By A. Cat (Koontz 2000)

We're Going on a Bear Hunt (Rosen & Oxenbury 1989)

Intermediate Titles

Deep Down Underground (Dunrea 1989)

Math-terpieces: The Art of Problem Solving (Tang 2003)

The True Story of the Three Little Pigs (Scieszka 1989)

Performance Strategies

Fluency Flexors

11

■ What Are They, Why Use Them?

Fluency flexors are short, focused exercises designed to flex reading muscles by reading, rereading, and rehearsing sentences or short passages to convey different meanings. When students read in choppy, halting bursts or come away from text with little understanding or memory of content, fluency flexors help them read smoothly and expressively while focusing their attention on meaning. Students read a sentence or brief passage using pacing, tone, inflection, and expression to convey various meanings. Following each reading, the group discusses what meaning was conveyed.

Experimenting with inflection, expression, and intonation using short pieces of text helps struggling readers and word callers focus on meaning in manageable chunks, encouraging deeper, more sustained reading. Ideally, the text of fluency flexors should come from books at readers' instructional level that they are currently reading and practicing.

■ Using Them in the Classroom

Use fluency flexors at the start of a guided reading session or to begin a reading workshop. As children gather, direct their attention to a sentence or short passage written on a transparency, the chalkboard, or sentence strips. (In guided reading, the text would come from the book the group is reading.) Read the sentence or passage, then have the students reread it in unison. After this, ask the students to read, reread, and practice the passage using appropriate expression, inflection, and intonation to signify meaning.

An alternative to practicing as a group is to give pairs of children a sentence or passage to reread and practice. They then share their "interpretive reading" with the class, and the listeners give feedback on what they understood. Finally, readers explain how their expression, intonation, and pacing reveal the meaning.

During reading conferences, you might also ask readers to pause and reread a certain sentence, passage, or paragraph "the way the writer meant it," discussing the rationale for their expressive interpretation.

Fluency Flexors in a Nutshell

1. Select a short text (one or two sentences) that might have different meanings depending on a reader's intonation, expression, and emphasis.
2. Write the text on a transparency, chart paper, or sentence strips.
3. Read the text aloud.
4. Read it in unison with your students one or more times.
5. Have students practice using appropriate intonation, emphasis, and inflection to convey various meanings. You might ask questions like these:
   - How does meaning change if we read as if we are scared, mad, or happy?
   - How do text signals guide our reading?
   - How does what we know about the story help us to read with appropriate meaning and expression?
6. As a group, discuss the meaning each reading conveyed.

Examples of Sentence Flexors

Brush your teeth.

Turn off the television and read a book.

Today you will mow the grass.

Keep your eyes on the ball.

Examples of Passage Flexors

Passages suitable to use as fluency flexors can be found in any text. Pick something that is smooth, rhythmic, and evocative and that lends itself to repeated reading and multiple interpretations. Two examples are offered below, but passages should generally be taken from books students are reading. When choosing flexors, try to select passages that provide opportunities for students to read "between the lines." Although meaning may vary, depending on how a passage is read and how it relates to the context of the story, the point is to help readers express their inferential understanding through an interpretive, fluent rereading of text.

In the passage below, from *Pictures of Hollis Woods* (Giff 2002), the author uses lyrical language and complex sentence structure. Teasing out the meaning may take several readings, but the effort is well worth it, especially if children are in the midst of reading this 2003 Newbery Honor book.

> "Drawing is what you see of the world, truly see."
> "Yes, maybe," I said, not sure of what she meant.
> "And sometimes what you see is so deep in your head you're not even sure of what you're seeing. But when it's down there on paper, and you look at it, really look, you'll see the way things are."

This passage tells so much about Hollis and her Aunt Beatrice, who encourages Hollis to "really look" at her drawings and through them to really see her perceptions of the world. The insights into character contained in this short passage help us understand Hollis' anger and realize how difficult it is to know why we feel and act the way we do. In taking a deeper look at her artwork, Hollis begins to know herself. Reading and rereading this passage flexor, we begin to connect events in the story and understand Hollis' actions and behavior.

The passage below is from the first page of *Sarah, Plain and Tall* (MacLachlan 1985). When read fluently, as the author intended, this passage reveals much about Anna and Caleb's history, the loss of their mama, and the mothering role Anna has taken on, sometimes begrudgingly.

> "Did Mama sing every day?" asked Caleb. "Every single day?" He sat close to the fire, his chin in his hand. It was dusk, and the dogs lay beside him on the warm hearthstones.
> "Every single day," I told him for the second time this week. For the twentieth time this month. For the hundredth time this year? And the past few years?

Connecting Them to Independent Reading

Children enjoy flexing their fluency muscles and will return to these sentences and passages many times. Once practiced, fluency flexor selections can be placed in a fluency center, along with sentence strips and markers: children can search for additional interesting flexors to write on strips and present to the group.

Following a fluency-flexing lesson, readers can search for interesting sentences or passages in their independent reading to reread, rehearse, and share with the group. They can also share how the passage relates to the story and what it reveals about the characters, plot, or setting.

Bringing Them Home

Providing appropriate, supportive reading activities for children and their families is an essential part of a comprehensive literacy program. Students often balk at reading to family members, particularly if they feel vulnerable or are struggling with the process. Sometimes, it is just too risky to fail in front of those we love most.

Sending home a few sentences or a short passage with instructions on rehearsing and encouraging expressive reading (and a few words about the importance of building fluency through such activity) supports fluency development and boosts reader confidence. Once rehearsed, fluency flexors guarantee success and fluent reading of text.

Using Them with English Language Learners

As English language learners read and reread text, they internalize the patterns and structures of written English. They also learn new vocabulary and concepts while experiencing them in specific contexts. Because other languages often differ in structure and word placement, using examples from a child's native language alongside the English version helps readers construct meaning and fully participate in the fluency flexor activity.

What to Read

Sources of fluency flexors are limited only by the literature available in your school and classroom. Although sentences can be taken from anywhere, both sentence and passage flexors should be at readers' instructional level (or a little above as repeated rereading will help them handle more challenging text). For the most part, passages should come from books children are already reading. Try to choose text that lends itself to different interpretations depending on how it is read aloud.

Primary Titles

Chickens Aren't the Only Ones (Heller 1981)

Koala Lou (Fox 1988)

Wilfred Gordon MacDonald Partridge (Fox 1985)

Intermediate Titles

Charlotte's Web (White 1952)

Sarah, Plain and Tall (MacLachlan 1985)

Pictures of Hollis Woods (Giff 2002)

12 | Radio Reading

■ What Is It, Why Use It?

Historically, stories and plays were read on the radio. This is still done today, though much less frequently. But classics, like the old Abbott and Costello tapes, are often replayed. Maybe you remember hearing about the radio panic of 1938, when Orson Welles presented a live performance of H. G. Wells' science fiction novel *The War of the Worlds*. In this version, the setting, the scene of a Martian invasion, was changed to Grover Mills, New Jersey. The performance seemed so real that New Yorkers ran outside to see the Martians landing their spaceships, and people across America called their local police and asked what safety procedures they should take. Talk about reading fluently with meaning and expression!

Today, radio reading is sometimes associated with radio stations whose mission is to broadcast the reading of newspapers and novels to the visually impaired and print disabled. Many of these readings are taped in advance.

Radio reading for fluency (Johns & Lenski 1997) can be treated either as a "live" performance or a prerecording. When students practice for radio reading, they learn to read accurately, quickly, and with expression. Accuracy becomes important and motivation increases when they realize someone will really be listening to them read.

▪ Using It in the Classroom

You can use radio reading in your classroom either as a live performance for an actual or pretend audience or as a taped performance.

Live Radio Reading in a Nutshell

This is easy to implement, although students need to practice their parts in order to read well. Here are the steps to follow:

1. Select something to read: a fiction or nonfiction book (chapter, passage, the whole thing), a play, a poem, a comic book, a child's writing, a radio script. The text should be challenging but should not frustrate your disfluent readers. If you think the material is too difficult for some of your students, prepare introductions and explanatory comments to help them.

2. Create a radio studio. Props, such as a table with an old microphone (or a facsimile) enhance the mood. A "set" like this helps students take the activity more seriously. Use "On the Air" and "Off the Air" signs to cue behavior. Children quickly learn that "On the Air" means only the reader should be heard!

3. Assign material and/or parts to specific students.

4. Let the students rehearse ahead of time, independently, with a partner, or at home with family members.

5. (Optional) Prepare sound effects: tapping a pair of shoes on the table suggests walking, exhaling simulates the wind, a knock indicates someone at the door. Sound effects will enhance the presentation and stimulate student interest, and almost any sound can be represented very simply.

6. Make certain that students understand their responsibilities. When they are "on the air" only the reader (and any prepared sound effects) should be heard.

7. Start reading. Encourage expression in reading so students will capture and keep the attention of their "radio audience."

Sometimes your radio play may be worth sharing with the whole student body, and it may be possible to go "on the air" over the school intercom system.

Recorded Radio Reading in a Nutshell

This is essentially the same as a live performance, but your set is now a recording studio. You'll need a tape recorder of some kind (one with a microphone is best). Extraneous noises will be heard on the tape, so everyone in the classroom must cooperate by being very quiet. An added benefit here is that you can do several takes if mistakes are made, and each repetition helps build students' fluency.

When the tapes are completed, you can share them with community organizations. Senior-citizen centers, nursing homes, day care for the elderly, and similar organizations will no doubt appreciate playing them. Before a tape is circulated, however, students should review and critique the reading. Suggest they focus on the smoothness of their reading and the appropriateness of their expression as they listen to their voices.

■ Connecting It to Independent Reading

During independent reading students can search for text to read on a radio show. For example, if the topic of a particular show is planets, students can search various sources for information on each planet. For a "story time" radio show, students can search for short interesting plots that contain a great deal of dialogue.

■ Bringing It Home

Willing listeners are very important as students practice for a radio show. Family members can help with enunciation and expression by first modeling for and then listening to their child. Parents and caregivers may also be able to tune in to suitable radio broadcasts. As children listen to these positive models they will pick up a number of pointers from the professionals.

■ Using It with English Language Learners

English language learners benefit by reading developmentally appropriate parts on the "radio," then listening to the taped "radio show" so they may listen to themselves and assess their progress. The script of the "radio show" should be available, enabling students to follow along, silently rereading as they listen to the tape. We recommend that when first introducing Radio Reading to English language learners, they be assigned parts that include repetition to ensure success and enthusiastic participation.

■ What to Read

Some of the following books contain segments of dialogue throughout and are especially suitable as a radio play. Others contain short expository sections relative to a particular subject.

Primary Titles

The Biggest Animal Ever (Fowler 1992)

Click, Clack, Moo: Cows That Type (Cronin 2000)

Thomas' Snowsuit (Munsch 1985)

Intermediate Titles

Bold and Bright, Black and White Animals (Patent 1998)

Cinderella: The Dog and Her Little Glass Slipper (Goode 2000)

Henny-Penny (Wattenberg 2000)

13 Getting into Character

What Is It, Why Use It?

When young children read in a monotone, their voices devoid of expression or inflection, they may be problem solving. Wading through unfamiliar text, they put intense effort into saying the words, with little left over for expression or interpretation. If readers are allowed to continue reading this way, there is a good chance that their understanding will be compromised. On the opposite side of the coin are the proficient word callers who skim the surface of reading, merely saying the words. Again, understanding is compromised.

Getting-into-character activities (Opitz & Rasinski 1998; Allington 2001; Johns & Berglund 2002) pull both these types of readers deeply into text, helping them plunge beneath the surface as they interact in substantive ways with meaning and content. Such strategies promote reader engagement through active involvement. As the name implies, students assume character roles as they read and reread text. First they read the text aloud or silently. They then reread it focusing on interpretation, attending to how characters might say or feel the words.

Using It in the Classroom

The three strategies described in this chapter are easily adapted for readers K–5. The latter two extend the model to interpreting a character's feelings and behaviors.

Assuming a Character in a Nutshell

As the name implies, assuming a character involves reading a character's dialogue confidently and expressively. Here are the steps:

1. Select a story made up almost entirely of dialogue.

2. Divide children into groups that match the number of characters in the story. (Include a separate narrator if necessary; if there is little narration, the children playing the characters can double up on the narrative sections as well.) With young children, two or three parts works best.

3. Have the groups read, reread, and discuss the text and perhaps complete an extension activity.

4. Have the groups share parts of their reading with the whole class.

5. Ask the class to discuss each "performance," saying what they understood and what meaning they took away from it.

Here's a classroom example. Sharon Roberts gives her first-grade partner teams the following directions as they prepare to reread *The Chick and the Duckling* (Ginsberg 1972): "Each take a part and read the story, then switch parts and read it again. After two readings, retell the story using your paper-and-Popsicle-stick puppets." She then lets the pairs of children structure their own partnership, together deciding which part they will read and who will begin.

Eddie and Patrick sit at a table, each holding a copy of the book, puppets of the chick and duckling on the table beside them. Eddie says, "What do you wanta be?" Patrick responds by saying, "I want to be squawk—squawk—squawk!" Eddie squawks in response, and the boys spend a minute playing with the puppets, making them dance, the popsicle sticks rapping a steady beat on the table. Finally Patrick says, "I read chick, you read duck," to which Eddie replies, "Okay. The first part is the chick part." He points to the floor. "We have to use this as water."

The boys read through the story, each taking his character's part. This is a familiar, patterned story, and they read it without miscues, using high, squeaky voices and putting their puppets through animated paces. At one point, Patrick's chick taps hard on the table and he cries, "Ow, I broke my leg," but otherwise they do not diverge from the words on the page.

Switching parts, they begin again, reading animatedly until the end of the story. They are preparing to switch parts and begin a third reading when Sharon reminds them that they should now retell the story. Patrick says, "I'll talk about the beginning. You'll talk about the middle. I'll talk about the end. Okay?" Then they begin, using puppets to reenact the story.

Assuming a character is particularly appealing to young readers like Eddie and Patrick. It can also be incorporated into intermediate readers' literature circles or other small-group reading activities.

Saying It Like the Character in a Nutshell

As students mature and move into silent reading, they often continue to read in a monotone. This hinders deep or thoughtful engagement in narrative, and readers "fail to understand that as plot develops, so do the characters" (Optiz & Rasinski 1998; Johns & Berglund 2002). Asking students to "say it like the character" prompts them to make inferences about characters' feelings and voices and to bring these inferences to bear on interpretive rereadings of text, incorporating intonation, inflection, and expression. In the process, they develop a feel for prosody, the rhythm and intonation of language. Here's how it works:

1. Have students choose a passage written from a particular character's point of view.

2. Ask them to reread the identified passage silently, focusing on how they think the character might say it.

3. Let students practice reading the passage aloud.

4. Ask students to read the passage orally, as they think the character would say and feel it, to their group or to the class.

5. Prompt the group or class to discuss what emotions readers were trying to show by asking such questions as:
   - Why are these feelings appropriate to this character?
   - How did the reader's voice and expression reveal meaning, character, and feeling?

Saying it like the character is similar to reading sentences as the author intended (see Chapter 11). Teaching these parallel activities in succession supports and reinforces spirited and expressive reading of text.

Being the Character in a Nutshell

Being the character (Allington 2001, p. 83) is a strategy in which readers select a character from a story or a biography and present a short solo performance as that character. Because they are pretending to be the character, they will need to adapt narrative text into dialogue. In preparing, students might use the character share sheet in Appendix F to collect background information and organize their thinking. They may also enhance their portrayal by using simple props or costumes. By the numbers:

1. Ask the students to choose a character to portray.

2. Have the students select segments of text on which to base a script.

3. Let students practice the script aloud.

4. Have students present their performance to the class, then share how they arrived at their interpretation.

5. Have the class react to the performance, giving their impression of the character and telling how they thought the interpretation was appropriate.

■ Connecting It to Independent Reading

All three getting-into-character strategies incorporate independent reading. Additionally, during reading workshop or sustained silent reading, children can be asked to search for interesting character dialogue and select a sentence or two to practice, share with the group, and explain what feeling they were showing and why.

Once students are familiar with any or all of the getting-into-character routines, they can pursue them in the fluency center. Provide a file of scripts and texts with strong character parts.

■ Bringing It Home

A simple and engaging assignment for readers of any age is to search texts at home (comic strips, cartoons, newspapers, magazines, books) for a snippet of dialogue to read, practice, and share. After they share it with the class, they can describe the text from which the snippet came and tell why they choose to read it as they did.

■ Using It with English Language Learners

Getting-into-character activities give English language learners a chance to hear, feel, and experience the interpretive readings of others as well as practice and rehearse their own. The sentences or short passages they read, reread, and share may be in English or in their first language. In the latter case, English speakers will get the opportunity to hear the rhythms and cadence of other languages.

■ What to Read

Any text, whether or not it contains dialogue, may be used to help readers get into character. Base your choices on your readers' needs and interests.

Primary Titles

Abigail Takes the Wheel (Avi 1999)

The Chick and the Duckling (Ginsberg 1972)

Days with Frog and Toad (Lobel 1979), and other titles in this series

Fables (Lobel 1980)

Good Night, Good Knight (Thomas 2000)

Nate the Great series (Sharmat various dates)

Small Pig (Lobel 1969)

Intermediate Titles

Children of the Gold Rush (Murphy & Haigh 2001)

Junie B. Jones series (Park various dates)

Kids of Polk Street School series (Giff various dates)

Magic Tree House series (Osborne various dates)

Tales of a Fourth Grade Nothing (Blume 1972)

The Great Brain series (Fitzgerald various dates)

Zack Files series (Greenberg various dates)

Because of Winn Dixie (DiCamillo 2000)

Reading Poetry

14

■ What Is It, Why Use It?

When we flex our fluency muscles, most of the time we are reading orally, and what better text for reading orally than poetry? Rehearsing and reading poetry aloud gives readers of all ages a shared experience with literature (Graves 1992; Larrick 1991). Many poems are short and lend themselves to repeated readings. With rehearsal, reading poems aloud enables children to feel the joy of successful fluent reading, encouraging attention to expression and intonation. Poems also lend themselves to different interpretations by different readers. How many times, after reading a poem silently, are we taken aback by the difference in sound and meaning when we hear it read aloud, especially by the poet herself?

■ Using It in the Classroom

In her luminous *Writing Toward Home: Tales and Lessons to Find Your Way* (1995) Georgia Heard asks, "Where does writing hide?" (10). Helping students find voice in their own writing and that of others is an important part of an educator's job. Once they have been introduced to the infinite variety of poems and poets, students enjoy the opportunity to read and write poetry, discovering voice in themselves and in others. There are many ways to incorporate poetry into literacy programs at all grade levels.

Many teachers use a "poem of the week" approach, whereby children read, reread, and sometimes memorize a new poem each week. Others designate a special time each day for reading and sharing poems. Still others introduce "poetry units," during which the class reads and writes poems for a specified number of weeks during the school year. Some classrooms host "poetry teas" and invite parents and others to come.

Poem of the Week in a Nutshell

This strategy can be adapted to all grade levels. The outline below is most appropriate for primary readers:

1. Select a poem, write it on chart paper, and hand out individual student copies.

2. Read the poem to the class several times, using appropriate expression and intonation.

3. Invite students to read along.

4. Read the poem in unison with the students one or more times until the reading is smooth and most children are participating.

5. Discuss the poem by asking:
   - What do you notice (words, rhymes, content, voice)?
   - Can you find words or lines you know?
   - What is the poet saying? What are the big ideas?

6. Read the poem with your students again, one or more times.

7. Have the students read the poem in unison, one or more times, using appropriate expression and intonation.

8. Ask the students to illustrate their copy of the poem and reread it silently.

Poetry Hour in a Nutshell

1. Together with your students, decide on a special time to read and share poems: an hour on Friday afternoon, first thing Monday morning, whatever works best.

2. Ask students to sign up to read a poem. (The reading may be a solo, a duet, or a small-group effort.)

3. Have students select, read, and rehearse their poem—alone, with a partner, or as a group.

4. Let students perform their selections during poetry hour. You may want to designate an emcee to keep a list of the order of readers and announce them. You might also invite other classes or special guests.

Before instituting a poetry hour, be sure you have shared all kinds of poems with your students, modeling expressive, interpretative reading. It is important to have a large and varied collection of poetry appropriate for all students' instructional and independent reading levels. Some teachers and students create charts with suggestions for how to read poetry and prepare for an oral performance. These charts are visual reminders of the importance of practice and attention to voice as children prepare to share with listeners.

Poetry hour can also be a time for learners to share their own poems with classmates. The same kind of practice and rehearsal should go into preparing to read one's own work.

Poetry Person in a Nutshell

A popular classroom job in many schools is the "poetry person." It is this person's job to select a poem to share with the group during morning meeting. Sometimes the poetry person asks another person to read the poem, but it is his job to make sure each morning begins with poetry.

Poet in Residence in a Nutshell

Often local poets are more than willing to spend a few days or a few weeks in a classroom, reading and writing poems with children. Nothing jump-starts a poetry unit more effectively than having a "poet in residence" at your students' side, helping them find their voice.

Writing Poetry in a Nutshell

As children work to create their own poems, they pay attention to rhyme, rhythm, pacing, and patterns. When writers compose, they pause often and re-read, listening to their voice and thinking deliberately about how they sound. For this reason, most any kind of writing, but especially poetry, enhances and strengthens reading fluency. Here are some ideas for encouraging your students to write poems:

- **Buddy poems** are written by pairs of students, each partner supplying a word for each line. These poems might be written as a response to something the children have experienced or read or they might pertain to a shared interest.

<u>Night</u>

Night	**night**	**night**
_____	_____	_____ **night**
_____	_____	_____ **night**
_____	_____	_____ **night**
Night	**night**	**night**

<u>Night</u>

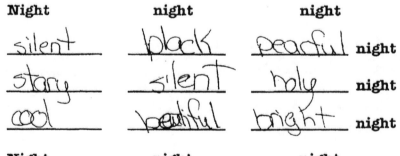

Night	**night**	**night**
silent	black	peaceful **night**
starry	silent	holy **night**
cool	beautiful	bright **night**
Night	**night**	**night**

Emily

FIG. 14–1 *Structured Poem "Night"*

- **Structured poems** are created using a simple scaffold like the one in Figure 14–1. The structure can be created by the whole group, then become part of center activities.

- **Pyramid poems** are fun to write and even more fun to read, the momentum building with each line. As the name implies, the poem begins with one word, then two, and so on until the poet decides he has reached the end.

- **Borrowed poems** appropiate the rhythms, patterns, and tone of an existing poem. Most kindergartners and first graders have created poems by borrowing the wonderfully simple structure of Bill Martin's *Brown Bear, Brown Bear, What Do You See?* (1983).

- **People poems** tell personal stories or explore the lives of historical figures. The simple structure illustrated in Figure 14–2 adapted from Finney (2003) can be varied to suit the age of the writers, the type of writing project, or the subject of the poem.

Line one:	Person's name
Line two:	Three or four adjectives that describe this person
Line three:	Five or six nouns that tell who the character is (brother, artist, friend, etc.)
Line four:	Cares about (three things)
Line five:	Feels (three emotions)
Line six:	Needs (three things)
Line seven:	Shares (three things)
Line eight:	Fears (three things)
Line nine:	Likes to wear (three things)
Line ten:	Wishes (finish the sentence)
Line eleven:	Lives (in name of town, on name of street, in name of state, or in a geographic locale like "by the shore")

FIG. 14–2 *People Poem Structure*

■ Connecting It to Independent Reading

A literacy or fluency center is an ideal place for students to read, reread, rehearse, and illustrate poems. Children will also read and rehearse poems independently in preparation for sharing with others. Creating excitement and interest about poetry sends readers to anthologies and poetry collections during independent reading.

■ Bringing It Home

Students can read and write poems at home, collecting ideas from family members and their surroundings. People poems can be written about or with family members. Children's parents, grandparents, and extended families can also be the subject of structured poems and "buddy poems."

■ Using It with English Language Learners

Poems are short and easily learned, and the rhythms and patterns support all readers, particularly those learning English. When English language learners listen to poems read aloud, they have repeated, meaningful exposure to the structure and cadence of written language. When they practice and rehearse reading poetry aloud themselves, they internalize these rhythms and structures, making them their own. Writing their own poetry according to specific structures supports English language learners in their efforts to use English words, concepts, and vocabulary in particular ways for particular effects.

■ What to Read

Poetry books for all ages abound. Some poems are funny, others poignant. Search for poems that will touch your students' hearts, roll off their tongues, and tickle their funny bones. Help them discover this magical kind of writing that lends itself so well to oral performance. A favorite basic resource book for poetry is the *Random House Book of Poetry* (Prelutsky 1983), but there are any number of excellent anthologies and collections from which to choose.

Primary Titles

A Bug in the Teacher's Coffee and Other School Poems (Dakos 1999)

Surprises and *More Surprises* (Hopkins 1984, 1987)

Nathanial Talking (Greenfield 1988)

Questions: Poems of Wonder (Hopkins 1992)

Weather: Poems for All Seasons (Hopkins 1994)

Seasons: A Book of Poems (Zolotow 2002)

You Read to Me, I'll Read to You (Hoberman 2001)

Intermediate Titles

All the Small Poems (Worth 1987)

Condor Magic (Hoopes 1997)

Everybody Needs a Rock (Baylor 1974)

Honey, I Love (Greenfield 1978)

If I Was in Charge of the World and Other Worries (Viorst 1981)

I'm in Charge of Celebrations (Baylor 1986)

Jamboree: Rhymes for All Times (Merriam 1984)

Miss Mary Mac All Dressed in Black (Hastings 1990)

19 Varieties of Gazelle (Nye 2002)

Poetry for the Earth (Dunn 1991)

Singable Texts

Down by the Bay (Westcott 1988a)

Five Little Ducks (Aruego & Dewey 1986)

Here We Go Round the Mulberry Bush (Hillenbrand 2003)

I Know an Old Lady Who Swallowed a Fly (Westcott 2003)

The Lady with the Alligator Purse (Westcott 1988b).

Old MacDonald Had a Farm (Alley 1991)

Seals on the Bus (Hart 2000)

Sitting Down to Eat (Harley 1996)

Skip to My Lou (Westcott 1988c).

Wheels on the Bus (Wickstrom 1985)

Take Me Out of the Bathtub and Other Silly Dilly Songs (Katz 2001)

This Little Light of Mine (Lisberg 2003)

15 | Readers Theatre

■ What Is It, Why Use It?

At a recent International Reading Association (IRA) convention, authors Avi, Bruce Brooks, Katherine Paterson, and Franny Billingsley gave a reading aloud theatre performance made up of excerpts from each author's books. Prior to the performance, they had planned and rehearsed how they would use each reading, who would read which sections, who would narrate, and who would speak each character's part. For the audience, one of the pleasures and surprises—aside from the opportunity to spend time with wonderful authors—was hearing the distinctive writing styles and voices inherent in each author's work. Performing literature by reading it aloud brings the qualities of voice, tone, and expression to the fore. It also fosters an awareness and appreciation of the unique voices and writing styles of the many wonderful authors of children's literature.

Readers theatre is an interpretive activity in which students read scripted stories, taking the parts of characters and narrator and using their voices to bring texts to life (Martinez, Roser & Strecker 1999). Unlike full-blown play productions, in which the lines are memorized, the emphasis in readers theatre is on reading. Students hold scripts and read, conveying the story through their vocal inflections, gestures, and facial expressions. Readers theatre doesn't require a whole lot of preparation. Students can read standing up or sitting down. They may occasionally wear a name tag identifying the character they're portraying, but beyond that, there are usually no props or costumes.

Preparing for a readers theatre performance, students reread the text many times, strengthening their fluency, confidence, and enthusiasm for reading. Participating in readers theatre, whether as performers or audience, boosts listening skills and builds a sense of community. Readers theatre is an easy, no-fuss opportunity for children to read with understanding and joy. Best of all, rehearsal and repeated reading ensures success for everyone.

■ Using It in the Classroom

Either fiction or nonfiction may be used for readers theatre. The material should be at or near the students' instructional reading level, as accuracy, pacing, and expression suffer when texts are too difficult. When using fiction, it helps to choose stories with meaningful characterizations that can be expressed through readers' voices rather than ones that contain lots of action. That said, almost any text can be adapted for a readers theatre performance.

The two variations that follow can be used with readers in kindergarten through grade 5, although instant readers theatre may be easier to implement with primary-age readers. Creating readers theatre scripts thrusts learners more deeply into the creative process, involving them earlier and letting them shape the material.

Instant Readers Theatre in a Nutshell

1. Choose a story or script at or near your students' instructional reading level. (Appendix G contains two simple scripts.) Whenever possible, students of any age should be involved in selecting the text for a readers theatre performance and encouraged to look for future scripts as they read independently.

2. Adapt the script or story text to accommodate the performers. (With younger students, consider performing as a whole class first, before assigning individual parts.)

3. Read the entire text to the students.

4. Hand out a copy of the text to each student and invite them to read along with you as you read it again.

5. Read a third time where you read narration and students read dialogue, then switch.

6. Assign parts to individuals, pairs, or groups. (Students might also choose roles themselves.) You can ask students to highlight their part or their copy if you haven't already done so.

7. Have the students rehearse at school and at home.

8. Have the students perform the piece for an audience made up of classmates, other classes, or parents.

Creating Readers Theatre Scripts in a Nutshell

A more advanced approach is to have students create their own scripts, either from published books or from scratch. Creating and then performing readers theatre scripts brings all the language arts—listening, speaking, reading, and writing—into play. As they adapt favorite stories into scripts, children focus on literary elements such as characters, plot, setting, structure, and tone. When students write original scripts based on favorite stories or nonfiction topics that interest them, they will visualize themselves saying and performing the lines flowing from their pens. The process might go as follows:

1. Have your class or smaller groups of students choose a topic or a published text on which to base a readers theatre script. (Biographies are good choices.)

2. Have the class or group discuss how they wish to proceed.

3. Guide the students as they prepare the script.

4. Have the class or group read the text in unison.

5. Decide as a group how the parts will be distributed and performed.

6. Have the students rehearse and perform the script.

7. As a class discuss the performance. What was the audience reaction?

Variations and Extensions

- *"I Never Thought I Could Be a Star: A Readers Theatre Ticket to Fluency"* (Martinez, Roser, & Strecker 1999) is a clear, five-day instructional plan for using readers theatre with second graders. Like all readers theatre variations, it includes many rereadings of the script so that all the readers are familiar and comfortable with all the parts. Rereading is key to any readers theatre activity.

- **Puppets** are simple props for extending readers' voices and gestures during readers theatre performances. Puppets can be as simple as paper bags or pictures mounted on popsicle sticks.

- **Turn a readers theatre performance into a television program** by performing it in a simple "television set." Students can also devise simple commercials between acts.

Connecting It to Independent Reading

Once students have performed several successful readers theatre productions, they will begin to see scripts everywhere.

"Let's do the Magic School Bus!"

"What about Maniac Magee?"

"If they can make a movie of *Holes*, we can do it as readers theatre!"

In the face of such enthusiasm, it should be easy to provide time and space for creating scripts, assigning parts, rehearsing, and performing. Encourage your students to base their interpretations on their understanding of stories and non-fiction concepts and ideas. Stocking a reading or fluency center with readers theatre scripts gives students an opportunity to read and reread them independently. When such centers are up and running, some teachers set aside a weekly time when readers can perform scripts practiced as a center activity.

Bringing It Home

Once readers theatre is implemented, students can take scripts home to practice. Listening to their children read and practice, parents are often pleased and surprised by their improved fluency. Students can also search home and local libraries for possible texts for future readers theatre scripts.

Using It with English Language Learners

Participating in readers theatre productions builds a sense of community and develops students' interpersonal, social, and collaborative skills. This is a good way to encourage English language learners to be full, active participants in classroom life. The structure of readers theatre, with its many rereadings and rehearsals, ensures a successful performance for all students, including those just learning English. English language learners need to hear many models of fluent reading in order to internalize what effective reading sounds like (Allington 1983; Hoffman 1987; Martinez, Roser, & Strecker 1999; Rasinski 2003) and what teachers mean when they say, "Read that with expression." By listening to their classmates, then participating themselves, English language learners experience fluent, expressive reading as both listeners and participants.

■ What to Read

Although almost any text can be adapted for readers theatre, you'll want to select texts that excite and motivate. Folk- and fairy tales are always popular choices. A great standby is Lobel's *Fables* (1980) because the stories are told with irony and wit (which adult audiences appreciate) and are so easily adapted as scripts. Most are only one page long. They can be photocopied, and the parts of the narrator and the characters highlighted. Harry Allard's Miss Nelson books are other perennial hits. Their strong characterizations and snappy dialogue make them appealing to performers and listeners.

Students in grades 3 through 5 especially enjoy performing fractured fairy tales like *The True Story of the Three Little Pigs* (Schieska 1989). Younger readers enjoy the rhythms and joyous repetition of such texts as *Chicka Chicka Boom Boom* (Martin & Archambault 1989) or *The Very Hungry Caterpillar* (Carle 1969). Nonfiction, if that's where your readers' interests lie, can also easily be adapted to readers theatre. Finally, there are many web sources for readers theatre scripts for students of all ages and reading levels.

Primary Titles

Chicka Chicka Boom Boom (Martin & Archambault 1989)

The Very Hungry Caterpillar (Carle 1969)

Good Night, Good Knight (Thomas 2000), and other titles in this series

Miss Nelson Is Missing (Allard & Marshall 1977), and other books in this series

The Birthday Cake (Cowley 1990a)

A Terrible Fright (Cowley 1990b)

Fast and Funny (Melser 1990a)

Help Me! (Melser 1990b)

Just Like Me (Melser 1990c)

Let Me In (Melser 1990d)

Poor Old Rabbit: A Play (Melser 1990e)

Sing to the Moon (Melser 1990f)

Well, I Never (Melser 1990g)

Cinderella (Trussell-Cullen 1999a)

The Miller Who Tried to Please Everyone (Trussell-Cullen 1999b)

The Three Wishes (Trussell-Cullen 2002)

Intermediate Titles

Alaska's Three Pigs (Laverde 2000)

The Frog Prince Revisited (Schieska 1991)

Herbie Jones and the Monster Ball (Kline 1988), and other titles in this series

Magic School Bus series (Cole various dates)

Magic Tree House series (Osborne various dates)

Snow White in New York (French 1986)

Stellaluna (Cannon 1993)

Strega Nona (de Paola 1975)

Three Cool Kids (Emberley 1995)

Three Little Wolves and the Big Bad Pig (Trivizas & Oxenbury 1993)

The True Story of the Three Little Pigs (Schieska 1989)

Zack Files series (Greenberg various dates)

Websites for Readers Theatre

www.scriptsforschools.com

www.aaronshep.com/rt

www.storycart.com

www.richmond.k12.va.us/readamillion/readerstheater.htm

www.readinglady.com

home.nyc.rr.com/teacherstools/readers%20theater.htm

www.fictionteachers.com/classroomtheater/theater.html

www.stemnet.nf.ca/CITE/langrt.htm

www.teachingheart.net/readerstheater.htm

www.lisablau.com/freescripts.html

www.suzykline.com

www.janbrett.com

Performing a Play

16

■ What Is It, Why Use It?

Plays are a different genre than readers theater. Readers theater is initiated through a complete story and does not require the same inferential skills as reading a play. Plays promote expression and require deep understanding of character through assuming roles and mimicking character expression. In plays, characters' thoughts are rarely voiced, so comprehension and expression must be implied through the dialogue and action. Putting on a play is an excellent way to build fluency because of all the rehearsals required to prepare for the performance. Practice allows students to gain greater control over their vocabulary. Portraying a character requires understanding of social interaction and provides an opportunity to mimic fluent expression.

As they prepare to "become someone else," students learn to interpret the dialogue, the situation in which the characters find themselves, and other dimensions of fluency not realized from a single reading. It is essential that students understand that the punctuation of the characters' speeches demonstrates how the lines should be expressed to convey the implied meaning.

Students get excited about being in a play. They practice with partners, they practice at home in front of parents, and they practice by themselves. Play rehearsals allow disfluent readers to become successful speakers of words.

■ Using It in the Classroom

The play you select should be developmentally appropriate for the students and at their instructional reading level. Remember, your goal is to build fluency: creating elaborate props and sets is time-consuming and will drain your energy. It's better that students work on a number of plays during the year than be limited to a once-a-year showcase.

Performing a Play in a Nutshell

1. Choose an appropriate play.

2. Allocate roles. You can assign particular students to particular parts, have children "audition" for the part they want, or let children choose their own parts. The easiest way to begin is to assign parts. This gives you more control.

3. Schedule rehearsal times, either for the whole cast or for the actors in a particular scene. You can also have the actors rehearse individually by:
   - Reading to themselves
   - Reading to themselves while facing a mirror
   - Reading into a tape and then playing it back
   - Reading while music is playing softly in the background
   - Reading to partners
   - Reading to a parent volunteer or teacher's assistant
   - Reading to you

4. Monitor rehearsals for accuracy and appropriate expression.

5. Keep the time spent in perspective. Your goal is to help children read more smoothly and expressively. Strive for better, not perfect.

6. Schedule the performance.

7. Have students write invitations to potential audience members (parents, other classrooms, school custodians, cafeteria staff, school administrators).

8. Have a dress rehearsal. Let the students decide if a second dress rehearsal is needed.

9. Present the performance. (Giving a second or third performance is even better.)

Variations and Applications

Using plays in the classroom need not be time-consuming or burdensome. Here are some simpler ways to proceed:

- *Skits,* or very short (often humorous) plays, require less preparation time, have fewer characters, and come to the point more quickly.

- *Puppet shows* also foster fluency (Allington 2001). Students can write a short puppet show script and create simple sock or stick puppets. Draping a sheet over a table, which the puppeteers work behind, creates a puppet theater.

- *Mimed narration.* Have a series of narrators read a story while other students act it out.

■ Connecting It to Independent Reading

Children can choose plays as part of their independent reading: many books and magazines include them. If you've narrowed down your choices of a play to per-form to two or three, ask students to skim them during their independent reading before voting for the one they like best.

■ Bringing It Home

Students can practice their parts at home, with their parents or family members as a captive audience. If props are needed, have the students write letters home asking to borrow the items. Encourage students to write their own skits and give impromptu performances for their neighborhood playmates or family members. This helps build oral language skills that will carry over into their reading.

■ Using It with English Language Learners

Pronunciation may be a factor for English language learners. If possible, have someone read their lines on a cassette tape or record them on the computer; they can then use the recording as a model.

■ What to Read

There are many play anthologies. Sometimes the plays in an anthology have a particular theme, like holiday plays. Any play you choose needs to be interesting, motivating, and engaging to the performers and the audience. When choosing plays to perform, look for length (short is better), appropriate reading level, simple props, repetitive language, and a decent plot.

Primary Titles

Easy-to-Read Folk and Fairy Tale Plays (Pugliano & Croll 1999)

Multicultural Plays for Children Grades K–3 (Gerke 1996)

The Three Little Pigs Puppet Play (Butterfield 1998)

Intermediate Titles

Plays for Young Puppeteers (Mahlmann & Cadwalada Jones 1999)

Showtime at the Polk Street School: Plays You Can Do Yourself or in the Classroom (Giff 1992)

What a World: A Musical for You and Your Friends to Perform (Mecca 1998)

Practicing and Applying Skills and Strategies Independently

Environmental Print 17

■ What Is It, Why Use It?

It is early morning in Joy Richardson's first grade, and the children are working at a variety of literacy centers. Pointers in hand, two students make their way along the perimeter of the room, reading the charts, poems, and stories that line the walls. Three other children work at the poetry center, where each line of the weekly poem has been written on a separate sentence strip. Using a chart paper version of the poem to check their work, these students assemble the strips in the appropriate sequence, plunking them into a large blue pocket chart. When they have finished, they read the poem in unison.

Both groups of students are meaningfully reading print they have practiced or helped create during literacy lessons and activities. Environmental print is text that covers classroom walls, text that represents the joint literacy endeavors of students and teachers that begin on the first day of school. Environmental print is a resource, a reference, and a reminder to children of their daily literate work. As they go about day-to-day activities, students pause and reread a familiar poem or story, building reading fluency and confidence. As they consult the word wall, they strengthen and solidify the rapid word-recognition skills that are necessary for fluent, accurate reading. In active, busy classrooms, environmental text records all of the following and much more:

- Classroom rules

- Poems

- Reminders of strategies for reading, writing, math, and other subjects
    - Spelling rules
    - Word-solving rules
    - "How to help the writer" chart
    - "What to do when I come to an unfamiliar word" chart
    - Grammar rules
    - Editing reminders
- Alphabet charts
- Homonym charts
- Compound word collections
- Name charts
- Interactive writing pieces
- Language experience pieces
- Modeled writing pieces

Creating texts to line classroom walls builds literate communities, as minds come together over what to write and how to write and read it. Helping create the classroom's print resources confers a sense of ownership that learners carry into all classroom pursuits. Although environmental print is more common and usually more profuse in primary classrooms, students in all grades benefit from the print found on walls, doors, shelves, and even ceilings.

▪ Using It in the Classroom

Walking through most elementary classrooms, one is inundated with print—word walls, alphabet charts, stories, poems, instructional posters, and songs. Often, the furniture is labeled, classroom rules and reminders are posted by the door, and a "books we love" bulletin board displays children's pictures and reviews of favorite books. As the year progresses, reading and writing strategy charts list children's ideas about the tools they need as readers and writers. The possibilities for environmental print are endless, dictated by the needs of your classroom, your students, and your curriculum. The following are just a few of the many ways teachers and students can create and use environmental print to build reading fluency.

Word of the Day in a Nutshell

From kindergarten to fifth grade, the word of the day is a highly effective activity that generates new environmental print each day. The five minutes it takes are fun, interactive, and predictable, allowing all students to participate. Model the procedures for two or three weeks at the start of the year, then turn the routines over to your students. One set of steps is offered below, but you should adapt and change them to suit the needs of your students and your literacy program.

1. Collect appropriate words, write them on small, word wall–size cards, and place them in a small box or container. (Mary Lee used a "treasure chest.") You can select words from many sources. Choose words that students will not instantly recognize, so that everyone participates in step-by-step word analysis. Here are some possibilities:
   - Words that follow letter-sound patterns your students are currently studying
   - Words taken from the students' work in literature, science, and social studies
   - Multisyllabic words that challenge all students' word-solving skills

2. Appoint a "wordsmith of the week." (Rotate this job weekly.) Each day this student selects a word from the box and writes it clearly on the whiteboard, chalkboard, or chart paper. No one may say the word aloud until the end of the activity.

3. The wordsmith then asks questions about the word. Questions will depend on the grade level and word-solving sophistication of the class. With younger students, questions might be:
   - What letters do you see? What sounds do you know?
   - How many consonants/vowels are there?
   - Are there patterns you recognize [consonant-vowel-consonant, consonant-vowel-consonant-vowel, etc.]?
   - Is there a part of the word you know?
   - Does this word remind you of another word you know?
   - How many syllables (or beats) does this word have?

   Questions for older students might include some of the above but also focus on unusual affixes, root words, and word origins.

4. The wordsmith divides the word into syllables and calls on individuals to read each syllable.

5. Finally, the wordsmith gives the signal and the group says the word in unison. By this time, every child knows the word and feels like a successful word solver.

6. The wordsmith posts the word on the word wall.

Word of the day allows all children to participate at their own level of expertise. More experienced word solvers often arrive at the word quickly. Because they cannot tell the word, their task becomes more analytic as they find a way to respond without giving the word away. Struggling readers lean on their classmates and the exercise itself, slowly blending and processing sounds and syllables as they are revealed. Word of the day generates excitement about word solving and words in general. After students have thoroughly analyzed each word, it is posted on the word wall, where it can be easily located and recognized.

Read the Room in a Nutshell

In this familiar and popular primary-grade activity, students, usually with pointers in hand, move around the room, reading the text on the walls—either pieces

FIG. 17–1 *Read the Room*

the students have helped create or familiar passages they have read and reread with expression and intonation. Older students also benefit from "reading the room" as a means of building reading fluency. Perhaps they can be asked to find a text to rehearse with partners and read aloud to the group. No matter the specifics, this activity makes print lining the walls more accessible to students, building and strengthening fluency skills and strategies. Most important, students love doing it. The steps are simple:

1. Have students (alone or with a partner) select a spot and begin reading.

2. Ask them to read, in order, all the print they encounter on the classroom wall (primary students may use pointers, rulers, highlighting wands, or their fingers to help them keep their place).

3. Later, have them share with the class or group something they discovered in their reading (types of words or phrases, for example).

Write the Room in a Nutshell

This is similar to reading the room, except children write their way around the room.

1. Give students (alone or with a partner) a clipboard and ask them to select a spot on the wall at which to begin.

2. Ask them to search the print on the wall for a particular aspect of language. Examples include:
   - Words in the same family
   - Words with certain consonant or vowel sounds and patterns
   - Unusual words or phrases
   - Sentences that can be read with many expressions or interpretations when taken out of context
   - Examples of parts of speech (nouns, verbs, adjectives, adverbs, etc.)
   - Examples of various kinds of sentences (statements, questions, exclamations)

3. Have the students read around the room, searching for appropriate examples and writing down the ones they find.

Word Walls in a Nutshell

Word walls can serve many different purposes depending on the grade level you are teaching, the needs of your students, and your curriculum. For kindergartners, word walls introduce the concept of *word* and list familiar high-frequency words (like *the*) and words that follow familiar patterns (members of the *at* family, for example).

No matter what words you place on the word wall, the following principles apply:

- *Word wall words should be displayed in alphabetical order* so that students can find them easily.

- *Word walls should be accessible*—visually at the very least, physically, if possible.

- *Words should be added in conjunction with the students,* not presented to them. This applies to every age level. If students are to own and use these important print resources, they must have a hand in creating them.

- *Word wall work should happen every day.* If students are to use and be aware of word walls as resources for reading and writing, the routines associated with them must happen daily. Whether words are added during a five-minute word-of-the-day lesson or at some other time, it should be a daily, regular routine. Older students can take a much more active role in finding words for the word wall in the topics and concepts they are studying in all their subjects.

- *Return to the word wall often.* Asking children to find words on the word wall or complete one of the extension activities that follow keeps these resources familiar and accessible.

- *Create word walls to serve different purposes,* such as names, science and social studies words, thematic words, vocabulary from novels and other texts. Such specialized sections can be taken down at the conclusion of a unit of study and filed where students can consult them for the remainder of the year.

Variations and Applications

There are so many ways in which environmental print can strengthen students' reading skills in all areas, including fluency. Search out whatever activities best support your literacy program and your students. Here are just a few suggestions:

1. *Word connections.* Ask students to complete this statement: "If I know this word _____ [from the wall], it helps me to know this word _____ [word that is somehow related orthographically, semantically, or syntactically]." Students can make these word connections on their own or with partners and then share them with the whole group. Connected words can also be posted on charts or sentence strips.

2. *Word sorts.* Word-sorting activities (see Chapter 23) make excellent use of environmental print as students collect and categorize words to share with their classmates.

3. *Word rings.* At the end of a unit of study, word wall words can be placed on rings and placed in a writing or word center.

4. *Portable word walls.* You can make excellent, "on the spot" use of portable word walls during guided reading, whole-class lessons and individual reading and writing conferences. The words are easily removed, rearranged, categorized, and sorted. Portable word walls bring words to students in accessible, flexible ways, inviting them to manipulate words and word patterns.

5. *Illustrating word wall words.* This is a wonderful extension activity for primary students, especially for students learning English as a second language. Tiny illustrations can be affixed next to word wall words to give readers and writers important clues as they reread.

6. *Personal word walls.* Older students can make personal word walls on sheets of paper or tag board divided into boxes, one for each letter of the alphabet. As they read a novel or content-area text, they select words from their reading that they want to be able to refer to easily. This is a particularly valuable activity for English language learners.

■ Connecting It to Independent Reading

The print lining your classroom is a resource that supports your readers' and writers' independent literacy endeavors. Center activities such as read the room and write the room use environmental print as texts.

■ Bringing It Home

As they develop as readers and writers, children notice environmental print everywhere—on their kitchen bulletin board or refrigerator, on billboards and signs, at the mall. Often, some of the first words children read are *McDonald's* and *Burger King,* accompanied as they are by familiar, visual symbols. Encouraging family members and children to create word walls at home takes advantage of students' excitement about words. The words can be posted on tag board, small corkboards, wherever families have space.

Students enjoy brainstorming with family members about the types of words they've learned about in school—homonyms, compound words, contractions. One morning, one of Mary Lee's first graders presented her with sixty-eight compound words! She and her dad had spent four hours the previous evening searching for these words, which she proudly displayed on a long piece of paper. Clearly, for some learners, excitement about words is contagious.

■ Using It with English Language Learners

Environmental print is an important resource for learners of English as they struggle to master thousands of words and their applications. Refer to classroom charts and word walls often, giving your English language learners specific strategies for how and when to use them. For example, you might ask them to:

- Use a word wall word in a meaningful sentence.

- Add a word to the word wall.

- Find a word they know and read it to a friend.

- Find certain kinds of sentences (statements, questions, exclamations) in the stories and modeled writing pieces that have been posted on the walls.

Whenever possible, a small picture beside a word on the word wall helps English language learners make semantic connections.

■ What to Read

The environmental print in your classroom is whatever you and your students create. It includes the poems, short rhymes, songs, and chants that you display in your classroom and that your students enjoy reading over and over again. As always, select texts that suit your students and your literacy program. *Phonics They Use: Words for Reading and Writing,* third edition, by P. M. Cunningham (HarperCollins, 2000) is one helpful resource.

18 Repeated Reading

■ What Is It, Why Use It?

After gathering her second graders on the rug in the center of her classroom, Mrs. Lee begins rereading a big book edition of *Drummer Hoff* (Emberley 1967). (She has also read the book yesterday and the day before.) She points to the words as she reads, and most of the students enthusiastically join in, especially during the last repetitive line, "but Drummer Hoff fired it off." After the final "Kahbahblooom," Mrs. Lee hands out small copies of the book for partners to read together. The book's vocabulary is not simple, but in the past three days students have internalized the rhyming pattern and repetition. Mrs. Lee walks around and listens as the pairs of students read with accuracy and expression, helping each other when necessary. She smiles inwardly as she asks several teams to be less expressive on "Kahbahblooom."

Rereading is used in classrooms to practice fluency (Fountas & Pinnell 1996), to correct miscues (Clay 1993), and to clear up misconceptions and gain deeper understanding (Harvey & Goudvis 2000). Rereading to practice fluency will eventually increase comprehension (Samuels 1997; Fountas & Pinnell 1996). In your initial reading, be sure you model all components of fluency. This ensures that when students reread they have some familiarity with the vocabulary and the proper expression.

Repeated reading as a fluency-building strategy was identified in the late seventies, researched and developed simultaneously by Jay Samuels and Carol Chomsky (Samuels 1997). Both researchers saw evidence that readers recognized more words on sight with repeated readings. The repetition builds familiarity with and automatic recognition of the words in the passage, and the words learned are then also recognized in other material.

Samuels' approach to repeated reading, in which he timed and recorded the readings, emphasized speed over accuracy. According to Samuels, when accuracy is emphasized the reader may become reluctant, losing her motivation as she becomes apprehensive about making mistakes. When a student is conscious of her miscues, especially when the miscues are being counted, she reads more slowly, without necessarily increasing her comprehension.

■ Using It in the Classroom

When rereading for fluency, you need to focus on accuracy, speed, and comprehension.

Rereading in a Nutshell

1. Select text that is interesting and at the students' instructional level. It can be a big book, a picture book, or a chapter book. (A chapter book is less cumbersome and intimidating if you divide the reading into sections.)

2. Read the material orally, with expression, as students follow along silently. Reread together again, if necessary.

3. Discuss any text signals.

4. Have students reread the material, either silently or orally with a partner.

5. If students are reading orally with a partner, observe their fluency.

6. Finally, have students discuss the reading collaboratively as a class.

Rereading can also scaffold the comprehension of expository texts. As a third-grade teacher, Nancy taught "The Sex Life of a Flower," or pollination. First, she put transparencies of the text and diagrams on the overhead and read students the information. Students then read the section on their own. Afterward Nancy led a class discussion to clarify information and verify the accuracy of details recalled.

Timed Repeated Reading in a Nutshell

Timed repeated reading is a strategy for readers who can recognize most words accurately but not quickly. Its emphasis on instant word recognition detracts from comprehension, as the reader unconsciously treats the meaning of what is being read as less important. But the focus on speed is appropriate for some students at this developmental level.

Timed rereading shouldn't be used with the whole class, only with those students whose progress is being hindered because they read too slowly. However, even students who read at a normal speed enjoy the challenge of timed rereading. Be sure to explain that increasing your reading speed is only beneficial if you can still comprehend what has been read. Help students understand that strategic readers are conscious of the purpose of their reading. They know when to read fast and when they need to slow down (adapted from Samuels, 1997; Johns & Lenski, 1997).

1. Select an interesting passage between fifty and two hundred words long (count the words). The reading level should be instructional or slightly above. (Even if the material is a little difficult, it becomes easier with rereading.)

2. Have the student cold-read the passage aloud, time the reading, and determine the words read per minute (WPM). Use this formula: number of words × 60 ÷ seconds required for reading = WPM (Johns & Lenski 1997).

3. Share initial reading rate with the student and make sure it is recorded. (Appendix H is a sample record sheet.)

4. Have the student practice reading on his own (or if needed, by listening to a recorded reading of the passage). Specify a number of times to practice, such as five. (While student is practicing, work with another student.)

5. Have the student reread the passage, again timing the reading.

6. Figure out the number of words per minute. Celebrate and record his progress.

7. Continue with another rereading if necessary.

8. Work with the student again using a different passage.

You can teach older students to time their own readings using a tape recorder.

Variations and Applications

- *Silent timed rereading.* Repeated reading can also be done silently. If this is being done independently, the student needs to note the time immediately before and after she completes the reading.

- *Tape-assisted rereading.* If a child makes a large number of miscues during the first reading, have her practice by reading along with a recording of the text read at the speed expected of the child's grade level. Once a student feels confident and is making fewer miscues, she should practice without listening to the tape.

- *Words correct per minute.* The timed rereading technique can be done along with a miscue analysis, counting only the words read correctly. The reading rate is then words correct per minute (WCPM) instead of WPM. If you are using WCPM, we suggest that you tape the reading. Students can then go back and hear their mistakes as you listen to the recording together.

■ Connecting It to Independent Reading

During sustained silent reading, ask students to choose a book they have already read. Tell the students to reread the book at least twice and see whether it seems easier the second time. In order to focus on comprehension, ask the reader if he noticed something new or different about the story during the subsequent reading.

■ Bringing It Home

Have the students do an experiment at home. Tell them to ask a family member to time them while they read silently for five minutes. Have them mark where they began and where they ended and count the number of pages they read in five minutes. Then they are to ask the family member to time them for five minutes again, while they reread the passage, beginning at the same spot they began before. Their goal is to read further the second time.

■ Using It with English Language Learners

The English language learner struggles not only with rapid word recognition, but also with the meaning and pronunciation of words and with enunciation. English language learners should listen to a tape recording of the passage as they practice. (Initially, passages should be kept short—around fifty words.) Once they have practiced a passage several times with the tape, they can practice on their own, going back to the tape if necessary. As they progress toward fluency, the passages should be lengthened.

■ What to Read

Choose passages for timed rereading that:

- Are at least fifty words

- Contain some words the student recognizes on sight

- Are slightly below, at, or slightly above the student's reading level, depending on the student

For short passages, articles or parts of articles from children's magazines (*Weekly Reader, Newsweek for Kids, Scholastic News, Ranger Rick,* and *Highlights*) work well. For older students, sections from a children's encyclopedia may be appropriate. Any poem of at least fifty words can be used.

Primary Titles

Charlie Needs a Cloak (de Paola 1973)

Frog and Toad All Year (Lobel 1976)

The New Hippos (Landstrom 2003)

Intermediate Titles

Dog Tales (Rae 1998)

The Legend of Bluebonnet (de Paola 1983)

No More! Stories and Songs of Slave Resistance (Rappaport 2002)

Wool Gathering: A Sheep Family Reunion (poems) (Wheeler 2001)

Attending to Text Signals

▪ What Are They, Why Use Them?

Text signals are signposts that help one read with appropriate expression and understanding. These signals include punctuation (commas, periods, question marks, exclamation points) and typographical variations like bold, capitalized, and italicized print.

Attending to text signals is an integral and important facet of making meaning. Teaching text signals highlights these important tools, placing them in the forefront of readers' thinking as they read aloud and silently. Attending to text signals helps readers with pacing, phrasing, and expression.

▪ Using It in the Classroom

In her classroom, Mary Lee called attending to text signals "following the rules of the road." The steps that follow can be used to teach any signal. When teaching text signals, first introduce the signal, such as a question mark, then give a clear, specific explanation about what it means to the reader: "when you see a question mark, raise your voice" or "with a question, raise your voice at the end of the sentence." Finally, provide ample practice and application in sentences and longer text.

Attending to Text Signals in a Nutshell

1. Select a signal you wish to teach.

2. Display sample sentences on sentence strips, on chart paper, on an overhead transparency, or in a big book. Ideally, these sentences should be pulled from texts your students are currently reading.

3. Read a sample sentence two times, once attending to the text signal, once ignoring the text signal. (For example: "When she heard the first yelp, Angel was at the sink washing the supper dishes" [Paterson 2002, p. 1].)

4. Ask which reading made the most sense, "sounded best," and what you did that made the difference. Eventually focus on the function of the text signal (for example, a comma signals a pause midsentence) and have the students reread the sentence again.

5. Have your students read the additional sample sentences, responding appropriately to the text signal.

Variations and Applications

You can codify your text signal lessons by having students create a chart outlining the function of each text signal. The chart should list the text signals, their functions, and sample sentences. The example in Figure 19–1 is adapted from many charts we have used as well as those suggested in Opitz and Rasinski (1998) and Johns and Berglund (2002).

■ Connecting It to Independent Reading

The most important reason for teaching text signals is so that readers will be able to identify and interpret them effectively on their own. As Kristen Vito says, "We've been stressing the role of punctuation in meaning making, and I've noticed my students coaching one another on how to use punctuation to read better." Anna, one of Kristen's first graders adds, "When you read with a buddy, there might be an excitement mark, and my buddy reminds me to read with excitement!" When students construct a text signals chart or discuss signals as a group, they are prompted to find examples in their independent reading.

SIGNAL	WHAT IT TELLS US	SAMPLE SENTENCES
Comma	Pause; read in chunks set off by commas to convey particular meaning.	Sarah, the character in the story, is plain and tall.
Period	Stop; longer pause.	The farmer drives a tractor.
Question Mark	Your voice rises at the end of the sentence.	Where are you going?
Exclamation Mark	Read with feeling!	Wait for me!
Underlined Text	Read with special emphasis.	This is <u>just</u> what I needed.
Bold	Read with special emphasis.	Martin, you **will** clean your room **now.**
Italics	Read with special emphasis.	The billy goat went over the bridge, *trip, trap, trip, trap.*
All Capital Letters	Read with special emphasis.	The billy goat went over the bridge, TRIP, TRAP, TRIP, TRAP.

FIG. 19–1 *Text Signals and What They Tell Us*

■ Bringing It Home

You can have students search for sample sentences illustrating text signals as homework. This will help parents understand the reading process and how they can support their children's literacy more effectively.

■ Using It with English Language Learners

Making English language learners aware of text signals helps acquaint them with the conventions and structures of written English. If learners are literate in their first language, you can compare punctuation and usage in the two languages. For example:

English: Will you play with me?

Spanish: ¿Jugarás conmigo?

■ What to Read

Any text can be used to focus on text signals. Ideally, it should be something the students are currently reading, most often at the students' instructional reading level. The text should be clearly visible.

Primary Titles

Frog and Toad series (Lobel)

Henry and Mudge series (Rylant)

Little Bear series (Minarek)

Intermediate Titles

The Same Stuff as Stars (Paterson 2002)

Any book by William Steig

Writing for Fluency

20

What Is It, Why Use It?

Writing involves a great deal of rereading. A student must reread what she has written in order to continue writing. Editing the work of a peer, which is a way to extend a student's own writing, requires that student first to read the work she's editing. Concepts and vocabulary are reinforced.

In order to build fluency through their writing, your students must be positioned to have a successful experience. An important part of that is having the means to be able to spell correctly, whether by checking with you, a spelling buddy, a dictionary, a computer spellcheck program, the word wall, or their personal list of tricky words.

The strong connection between reading and writing, the transference from encoding to decoding and back again, is key to building fluency through writing. Students should read orally and silently as they write and rewrite. Not rereading what one has written almost always results in error and confusion. A quick-write or a journal entry may never need to be reread, but in order to rewrite a piece the student has to have reread the current draft.

Using It in the Classroom

There are many ways you can incorporate writing for fluency in your daily classroom activities. First give your students an authentic reason to write, followed by a motivating reason to read and reread. Many kinds of student writing can be read aloud to other students or parents: a readers theatre adaptation of a story, a poem at a poetry tea, a story to a partner, a book report.

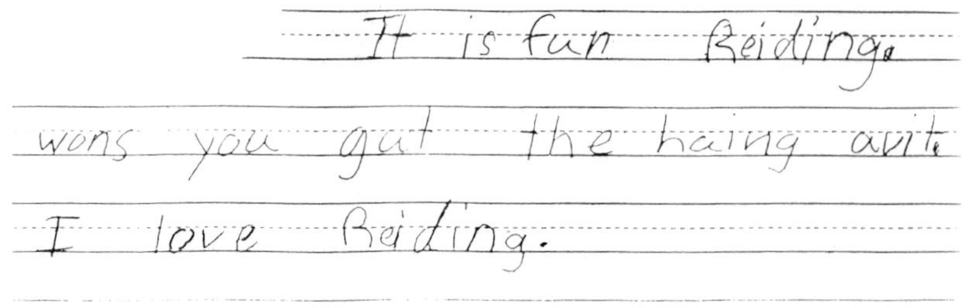

It is fun Reiding.
wons you gut the haing avit.
I love Reiding.

FIG. 20–1 *I Love Reading: Student Writing Sample (It is fun reading.*
Once you get the hang of it. I love reading.)

Keep in mind three "rules" of writing for fluency:

1. Make sure students can easily find the correct spelling of words they want to use.
2. Include a component that forces students to reread their work.
3. Encourage students to read their work orally whenever possible.

Writing for Fluency in a Nutshell

Modeled writing can be used to teach a particular type of writing, like a first-person narrative, a description, a letter, or an essay. Modeled writing is heavily teacher directed, but the students observe and approve the flow of the material as it develops. The reading and writing connection is so strong that learning transfers from one to the other naturally.

Here's how it works:

1. Chose the type of writing you want to model.

2. Compose a piece of writing in that style on a transparency or flipchart, explaining your thinking as you go.

3. Discuss both content and form. (For instance, you might begin a letter by writing, *It has been awhile since I have last written. I have been so busy.* Go back and reread these two sentences out loud and say "Gee, I say that I have been busy, now I need to tell my friend what I have been doing to be so busy.")

4. Write a few more sentences supporting what it is you are doing, again explaining your thinking regarding form and content.

5. When you have finished, reread the entire piece orally.

6. Have your students reread the text, first as a class, then with a partner and/or silently to themselves, giving them more practice with the written words.

Language Experience in a Nutshell

Another approach to writing is to have your students document a learning experience. You become the scribe, writing down something the students recount in their own natural language. There is some controversy about how exact you should be. If your goal is to build fluency, it's best to refine their oral language into standard English, then reread the information and get them to approve it as written. The steps here are:

1. Have your class participate in an activity that they can subsequently write about (going on a field trip, baking cookies, conducting a science experiment, learning a craft).

2. Stand at the blackboard or a flipchart and prompt your students to write about the activity: "What did we do today? What's a good way to start our narrative?"

3. Write down sentences as students volunteer their thoughts. If something is suggested out of sequence, ask that student to hold the thought, continue with other suggestions in the correct order, and ask for the detail when it's appropriate.

4. Conclude the piece by asking, "What is a good way to end our narrative?"

5. Reread the narrative in a variety of ways: ask the class to read it in unison; ask students to read the sentences they contributed; have students read the piece to a partner.

Some students may need more detailed small-group work:

1. Choose a limited number of words (five or six) from the narrative and put them on word cards.

2. Hold up a card. Have the students find the word in the learning experience narrative and read the sentence in which the word appears.

3. Have students think of another sentence using the word.

4. Write the sentence down on a new chart or the blackboard.

5. Have students read the new sentence.

6. Continue this process with the remaining word cards.

Writing to a Character in a Nutshell

Writing a letter to a fictional or historical character allows students to share their understanding of the story and use some of the vocabulary they encountered. You should model this activity before asking your students to do it independently.

1. Read a book that has an interesting plot and a small number of main characters.

2. Discuss the plot and the characters' feelings with your students.

3. Discuss with the class things they might want to write to these characters. Ask students what words they might want to use and write the words on a chart that everyone can see. Be sure to include the spelling of the characters' names.

4. Tell each student to pick one character to whom they want to write a letter.

5. Review the components of a letter and have the students write their letters.

6. Work with students in preparing final drafts of the letters.

7. Put the letters in a notebook for the class to read during independent reading. (This notebook can also be sent home to be shared with family members.)

■ Connecting It to Independent Reading

Children love to read books the class has authored. Language experience pieces and modeled writing can be saved to be read over and over again for pleasure during independent reading. (The charts can be affixed to hangers with clothespins and hung on a portable clothes rack.) Students' writing can also easily be comb-bound into a book or put into plastic sleeves and collected in a binder.

■ Bringing It Home

There are many exciting ways to get children to write at home. Suggest that family members encourage their children to write thank-you letters or assign a thank-you letter as homework. So that students can practice procedural writing, have them make something or perform an activity with a family member and then write down the directions. (The student can then share the directions and the product or activity with classmates.) Or have your students interview a family member and then publish these interviews in a class newsletter.

◼ Using It with English Language Learners

Writing is usually more difficult than reading for any student. If your English language learners are literate in their first language, allow them to fill in the "gaps" by writing unknown words in their native language. Together, you can make the appropriate translations in a conference. If they are not literate in their first language, have students draw a small picture to remind them of what they want to say. Again, help them communicate their thoughts in English in a conference.

◼ What to Read

You can use the events in a book as the basis for a language experience piece. Stories about familiar experiences like having chicken pox or going to the dentist are wonderful catalysts. Modeled writing can be reinforced with published examples.

Primary Titles

Arthur's Chicken Pox (Brown 1994)

Dear Rebecca (Craighead 1993)

The Doorbell Rang (Hutchins 1986)

The Kettles Get New Clothes (Dodds 2002)

Intermediate Titles

Josie's Troubles (Naylor 1992)

My Rotten Redheaded Older Brother (Polacco 1994)

Only Opal: The Diary of a Young Girl (Cooney 1994)

Shelf Life (Paulson 2003)

21 | Humorous Text

■ What Is It, Why Use It?

"Why can't it rain two days in a row?" "Because there is a night in between."

Answering that riddle when she was in fifth grade won Nancy a prize from a local radio station. Jokes, riddles, and comic strips are perennially appealing. How often, during free reading time, we find students reading riddles or jokes to one another. Why? Because they're fun! They are some of a classroom's most underrated texts.

In third-, fourth-, and fifth-grade classrooms, riddle and joke books are student favorites. Garfield and Calvin and Hobbs books rarely sit on the library shelves. Characters in humorous text appeal to children. The vocabulary is usually known or easily learned. The pieces are short and fun to share with classmates. Comic strips are short, use unusual and varied vocabulary, include picture cues, and rely heavily on inferences. Readers make connections, strengthen their comprehension, and are motivated to read more and read more deeply (Norton 2003; Marchionda 1996). Short humorous texts are ideal for building fluency. Because they are not cumbersome, the reader can focus on comprehension.

The reader also often depends on prior knowledge to "get" the joke. He retrieves information from the mind's "file folders" (Cooper & Kiger 2003), connecting the old knowledge to the new information. The more stored information a reader has on a particular topic, the easier it is for him to connect. Sometimes he may have a huge amount of background on a particular subject, but one missing piece causes confusion and stops a connection.

Keene and Zimmerman (1997) categorize three types of connections: text-to-self, text-to-text, and text-to-world. References to everyday life usually prompt readers to connect those experiences to what has happened or is happening in their own life (text-to-self). *Family Circus* humorously portrays the rewards and difficulties of living in a household with small children. *Arlo and Janis* is themed on such issues as teenage angst, dreams, and romance. *For Better or Worse* makes us laugh at the complications of dealing with elderly parents, teenagers, college students, married children, and grandchildren. Comic strips also often trigger connections to other literary works (text-to-text): seeing a wolf, we instantly think of Little Red Riding Hood. In still other instances, we may relate to occurrences in our friends' lives, a place traveled, or a political situation (text-to-world). In making all these connections, readers rely on prior knowledge to form a clearer understanding of what is being read.

■ Using It in the Classroom

Children love to laugh. It's good for their health, and it's good for your health, too. Jokes, riddles, and comic strips are a great way to model comprehension strategies. Only you can decide the best way to incorporate humorous text into your classroom. Some teachers rely on humorous text to fill those five restive minutes just before lunch. Others reward their students with a few minutes during the day in which to share jokes. Still others stock the classroom library shelves with all kinds of humorous text for students to enjoy whenever they have time to read independently.

You can find time for humorous text in a variety of ways:

- Institute a joke of the day.

- Designate a weekly, biweekly, or monthly time slot when children share humorous text.

- Incorporate it into your curriculum to help students understand important concepts.

Sometimes humor is lost on students because they don't know the vocabulary or have no connection with the topic. (For example, think of the political cartoons printed in many social studies and history textbooks.) Recently Nancy taught memoir writing to a sixth-grade class. She began her lesson with a cartoon about a young adult who refuses to throw away old pairs of shoes. In the cartoon, the character is saying, "Some people write their memoirs, I throw mine in the bottom of the closet." Two people in the classroom laughed—Nancy and the classroom teacher. Nancy immediately realized two things: these young students didn't save shoes and probably didn't know what a memoir was.

If a joke is not readily apparent to students, some explanation will be necessary. You need to make certain that students grasp the background and the social circumstances relative to a cartoon if they are going to be able to make sense of it.

Humorous Text in a Nutshell

1. Collect jokes, riddles, or comic strips at your students' reading level.

2. Using an overhead, share a few of these jokes, riddles, or comic strips with the class:
   - Discuss the text features and how this affects the reading.
   - Model the reading for the students using proper expression, intonation, and appropriate pauses.
   - Ask students to explain your reading: the tone, expression, and the pauses.
   - Discuss the meaning of the joke. If necessary, explain the punch line.
   - Have the class read the humorous text on the overhead in unison.

3. Give students their own jokes to read and discuss in collaborative groups.

4. Walk around and listen. Spot check for understanding.

Inner/Outer Circle in a Nutshell

This activity allows students to practice purposeful oral reading.

1. Make sure each student has a joke, riddle, or comic strip to share.

2. Let students practice reading their text using proper expression, intonation, and pauses. Walk around and listen to as many as possible, focusing on the students who are having problems with fluency.

3. Divide the class in half. Designate one half the inner circle, the other half, the outer circle. The students in the inner circle should face the students in the outer circle. If there is an odd number of students, join the smaller circle yourself so everyone has a partner.

4. Have the students read their humorous text to their partner.

5. Have the inner circle move one person to the right (clockwise), so that everyone has a new partner. Have them read their text again.

6. Repeat until everyone again faces their original partner.

Variations and Applications

- **Wacky wall.** This spin-off of a word wall is a collection of humorous texts that the teacher and/or students want to share. This is a wonderful center or "reading the room" focus.

- **Create a comic strip.** Select a humorous text (such as the chapter "Uncle Feather," in Judy Blume's *Fudge-a-Mania* [1990], in which the boys have a hilarious time trying to convince an elderly woman that their lost Uncle Feather is a bird) and have your students use it as the basis for drawing and writing their own comic strip. Students can cut large white construction paper in half lengthwise and fold each half into four or five sections. (The completed comic strips can be posted on the wacky wall.)

- **Comic capers** (Marchionda 1996). Use comic strips to:
  - Teach or reinforce vocabulary
  - Reinforce content information
  - Aid in understanding inference
  - Teach text features such as quotes within dialogue

■ Connecting It to Independent Reading

Centers and sustained silent reading are excellent opportunities for students to read humorous text. Short texts made up of jokes and riddles are less intimidating. Classroom collections should include many books or scrapbooks containing jokes, riddles, and comic strips children enjoy. Remind students that jokes are meant to be read with expression, sometimes with exaggerated intonation and a pause before the punch line.

■ Bringing It Home

Want some positive PR (parent relations)? Have students bring in humorous text from home. Ask them to read the newspaper and their children's magazines looking for jokes, riddles, and comic strips to share. Students can also gather jokes from books at their local public library. (On-line jokes are usually not appropriate for children.) Students can practice reading their jokes to their parents, siblings, grandparents, babysitters, friends, and neighbors before sharing them with the class.

■ Using It with English Language Learners

It is often difficult for English language learners to grasp the meaning of humorous text. What is funny in one culture may not be funny in another, so the comical meaning of a joke, riddle, or comic strip may be lost or misinterpreted. Also, humor often relies on idioms, sayings, or the double meaning of words (puns)—the very features of English that cause the most problems for English language learners (Jimenez 2003). For example, consider this ageless elementary school riddle: "Why did the man throw the clock out of the window?" "To see time fly." English language learners may not understand that "time flies" means that time seems to be going by quickly, but they may nevertheless laugh at the mental image of a clock being thrown out the window. Observing the laughter, a teacher might easily assume the English language learner understood the riddle when in actuality he did not.

English language learners must be taught multiple meanings of words and phrases. They also need numerous exposures to these words in context. Explaining and discussing the double meanings of words used in riddles is a fun, supportive way to increase English language learners' knowledge of word meanings. Reading and discussing books like *Amelia Bedelia 4 Mayor* (Parish 1999), in which the double meanings confuse even the characters, also fosters an awareness of idiomatic expressions and words with multiple meanings. Encourage older students to consult a dictionary.

A third grader once told Nancy this riddle: "What does a frog say?" "Time is fun when you're having flies." Is it any wonder some English language learners find humorous text a struggle?

■ What to Read

Humorous text in the classroom needs to be age appropriate. What a kindergartener will laugh at and what a fifth grader finds comical are usually quite different things. Simple texts in which students can figure out the inferences are best.

Primary Titles

The Mega Joke Book for Kids (Browning 2000)

Pigs, Giggles, and Rabbit Rhymes (Downs 2002)

Riddles and More Riddles (Cerf 1999)

Intermediate Titles

Animal Quakers: Jokes for Kids (Birtle 1998)

The Everything Kids' Joke Book: Side-Splitting, Rib-Tickling Fun! (Dahl 2002)

Joke Book (Lewman 2000)

22 | Series Books

■ What Are They, Why Use Them?

Growing up we both loved the Box Car Children and Nancy Drew, but we weren't fussy—we read the Hardy Boys, too. Mary Lee's sons loved the Great Brain, Redwall, and Freddy the Pig series. Nancy's oldest son got hooked on Choose Your Own Adventure books; her next son devoured the Goosebumps series. More recently her youngest son lived with his head submerged in J. K. Rowling's long-awaited *Harry Potter and the Order of the Phoenix* (2003). Like so many children, this fourteen-year-old had not voluntarily read a book since the summer he started and finished the first four Harry Potter books. Series books are serious motivators for children and adults; it is worth the effort to get them hooked. It has been shown that series books improve student attitudes toward reading, increase the amount of time they spend reading voluntarily, and increase their fluency (Worthy & Broaddus 2002).

Allington (2001) defines series books as books that either (1) have continuing characters (Harry Potter) or (2) are predictable in plot and story line (Choose Your Own Adventure). Series books are effective in building both fluency and comprehension skills. Like the sitcoms some adults set their watches by, series books have familiar characters and settings and predictable plots. These components, along with natural dialogue, enable less fluent readers to practice their word recognition and inferencing skills (Allington 2001; Opitz & Ford 2001). The high comfort level associated with series books builds reader confidence.

Familiarity with the characters helps readers form accurate predictions and follow the plot.

Unfortunately, many series books have a reputation as not being "quality" literature. However, children are more likely to apply key comprehension and reading strategies to text they are eager to read (Jackson & Davis 2000). If our goal is to increase our students' fluency and reading enjoyment, any text they like is beneficial.

Students' interest in series books is often triggered by their peers and by marketing promotions, not by their teachers. For instance, the popularity of The American Girls Collection and its related paraphernalia is primarily generated outside the classroom: young girls' friends, the media, even their parents, are all talking about the books, and they eagerly choose their own favorite character. A new Harry Potter book is a media-driven event that gets young and old reading.

◼ Using It in the Classroom

This same phenomenon can take place in your classroom. You can introduce a new series as you would a new author, through a read-aloud. Once your students are intrigued with the plot and characters, give a short talk about other books in the series. (The books need to be at the right level of difficulty—not too hard, not too easy.)

Because many series books use a lot of dialogue, they can be easily adapted to readers theatre. They can also be implemented easily and used effectively in guided reading. The initial scaffolding may enable disfluent students to enjoy other books in the series independently. Students who are reading different books in a series can discuss the characters' motivation and actions within the context of the various plots.

Series Books in a Nutshell

1. Directly teach necessary vocabulary.

2. Build background knowledge. Even a simple Frog and Toad story like "Cookies" (Lobel 1970), which is about dieting and willpower, requires some background knowledge to understand. Although it's hard to think anyone doesn't know about dieting, this—and even more so, willpower— may not be a familiar concept to young children.

3. Have students silently read small sections. After each section, check for clarification. For instance, after the appropriate section in "Cookies" you might ask, "How did Frog and Toad feel when the birds ate the cookies?" Some other examples of clarification questions are:
   - What did you think when ____ happened? What made you think that?
   - Did you think it was fair when ____ happened? Why or why not? What made you think that?
   - What does this event tell you about the character? What made you think that?
   - What could [character's name] have done differently? What made you think he or she could have done that?

4. Institute purposeful oral reading/rereading. Workable prompts are:
   - "What made you think that?" This leads students to find the passage in the text that supports their answer and read that portion of the text orally.
   - "What did the character say to show he felt that way?"
   - "Read your favorite part of the story out loud."
   - "Read the most important section of the book to your partner."

Variations and Applications

- *Institute series incentives.* Students love a competition, so challenge your class to read every book in a particular series. Post the series titles on a bulletin board. After a student reads one of the books, she can tack a summary of it next to the title. (Younger students can draw a picture of a scene in the book.) Once all the books have been read, celebrate in some way connected to the series. For example, after reading the Winnie-the-Pooh books, one class of second graders made sock puppets of their favorite characters.

- *Institute series discussions.* Have a group of children each read a different book in a series and discuss how events in one book parallel events in another. You can also have the group make a chart summarizing the characters, plots, and resolutions of the various books.

- *Write your own miniseries.* Decide on a character (create one as a class or pick one from a published story). Have each student (or pair of students) write a story about this character. String the stories together to make your own miniseries.

Connecting It to Independent Reading

Encourage your students to read series books on their own. Giving a book talk about a series introduces students to the characters and plots. Reading from one aloud models the tone and style of the author. Students can make a "commercial" encouraging others to read their favorite series.

Bringing It Home

Most parents will be delighted to find their son or daughter has a favorite series. Once students are hooked on a series, encourage family members to give the volumes as presents or check them out of the local public library. Assign fun projects related to a series as homework. For instance, one Frog and Toad book features a to-do list, and you could have students write a list of their own with a family members' help (see Figure 22–1). Or students and a family member could make the cake that is about to be baked at the end of "Cookies."

Using It with English Language Learners

Series books can help English language learners acquire oral vocabulary useful in their everyday life. The humorous or interesting events in series like Frog and Toad, the Fudge books, or The Babysitters Club mirror things that happen to everyone.

It's important to assess English language learners' prior knowledge. As the saying goes, "Assume nothing." Bacon and eggs or even cereal is not normal breakfast fare for most Asians. Nancy lived on Guam for a short time. Once when she was peeling a potato, five-year-old Karla asked, "What is that?" Told it was a potato, she followed up with, "Can I have a taste?" "Sure," said Nancy, handing her a piece. "But we usually cook it first."

What to Read

The criteria for choosing series books are student interest, student ability level, and book availability. Choose a series that will serve a designated purpose in your classroom and that is age appropriate. If you are planning to read a series as a class project, you'll need enough books to go around. If you introduce a series you want your students to read independently, choose carefully. An entry in A Series of Unfortunate Events (Snicket various dates) makes a great read-aloud,

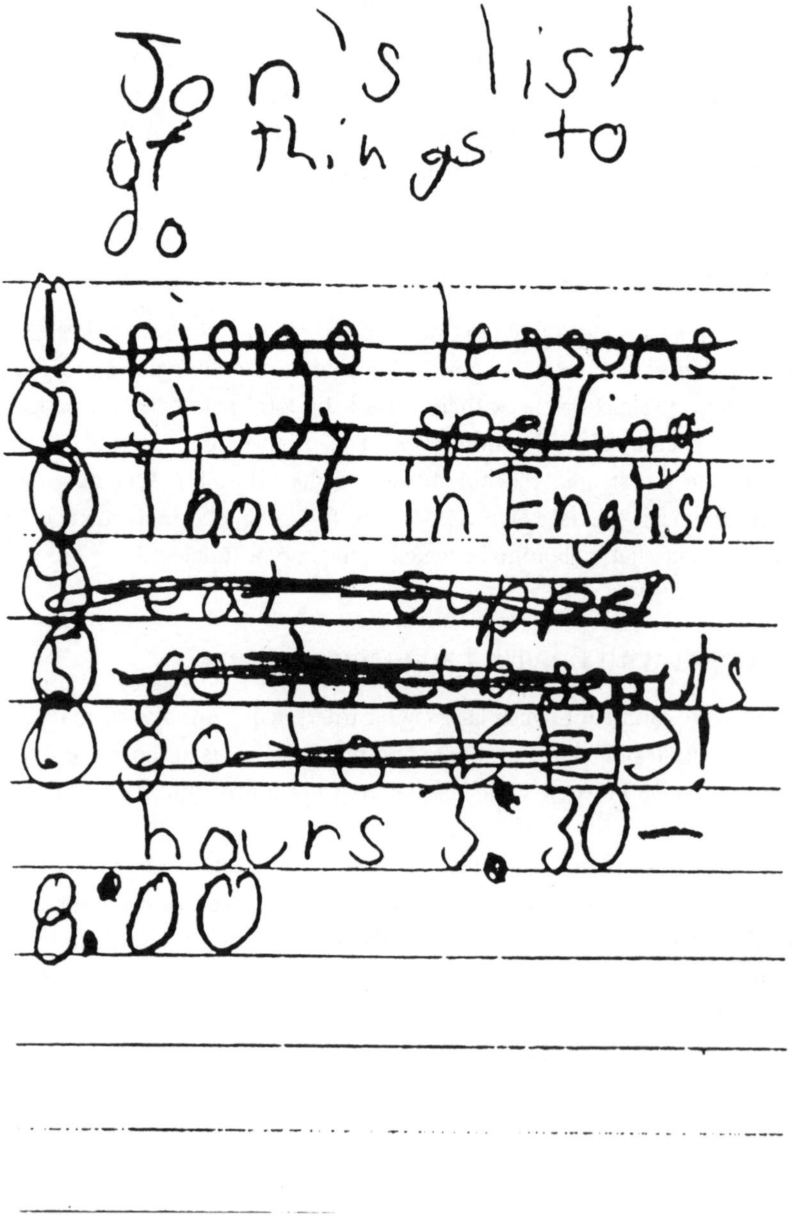

FIG. 22-1 "To-Do List," Student Writing

but the books can be difficult for students struggling with fluency to read independently.

Primary Titles

Berenstain Bears series (Berenstain & Berenstain various dates)

Frog and Toad series (Lobel various dates)

Magic Tree House series (Osborne various dates)

Zack Files series (Greenberg various dates)

Intermediate Titles

Babysitters Club series (Martin various dates)

Goosebumps series (Stine various dates)

Harry Potter series (Rowling various dates)

Working with Words

Sorting Words

23

■ What Is It, Why Use it?

Readers must be able to recognize words easily, analyze them, think about their meaning. In word sorts, students allocate words to different categories based on letter patterns and sounds (Cunningham 2000) and sometimes also on meaning. The words are written on slips of paper or index cards so that they are easy to manipulate. Initially the number of onsets (beginning sounds) and rimes (ending spelling patterns) should be kept to a minimum. For example, take the words *pat, cat, rat, hat, hot, cot, pot,* and *rot.* There are two important categorical responses to these words, either by the spelling pattern of the short *a* or *o* sounds followed by *t* or by the beginning consonant sounds. More advanced students can work with more spelling patterns and therefore more grouping possibilities. The words *catch, shack, patch, sick, pipe, kick, shirt, ship, mark,* and *shape* can be grouped by beginning, middle, or ending sounds; by whether or not they have a vowel consonant silent *e* pattern (VCe); by whether or not they have *r*-controlled vowels; and by whether or not they contain blends. Building fluency requires going beyond these simple patterns and using words the child does not automatically recognize.

■ Using It in the Classroom

Using word sorts as a prereading vocabulary activity or as a postreading reinforcement activity enhances students' comprehension by expanding their knowledge of what words mean and how they are used and by helping them recognize words quickly. It reinforces their ability to recognize spelling/sound patterns, pronounce less phonetically approachable words, and acquire a bigger vocabulary. Whenever possible the words should come from their current reading. However, remember to choose the words with care. You don't want this to be an exercise in frustration!

Word Sorts in a Nutshell

1. Choose a series of words for your students to sort. Using words from trade books and textbooks the students are reading helps integrate this activity into the classroom. The following words are from *The Snowy Day* (Keats 1963):

crunch	tracks	snow	stick	smacking
climbed	slid	while	dream	smiling

2. Initially, in an effort to build fluency and enhance comprehension, tell students to sort the words any way they can and then explain how they did so. (Using the words above, students might sort by beginning letter or blend, vowels or vowel sounds, words with *ck,* words with five letters, and so on.) Have students read their word groups out loud to you or to their partner.

3. Specify categories into which students are to sort the words. This directed sorting is often based on the meaning of the words. For example:
   Things you see
   Things you hear
   Things you can do

4. Make sure students understand the sorting directions, and assess their word knowledge.

5. Have students share their groupings orally with a partner.

6. Specify new sorting categories if appropriate and if time allows.

Each sorting direction should be given separately, and answers should be discussed. As words are used over and over again, students will internalize how they look and what they mean.

Phrase Sorts in a Nutshell

This adaptation of word sorts helps students group words together as they read the text. Use phrase sorts with students who recognize the majority of the words in the text but are obviously struggling with the flow of reading.

1. Select phrases that can be sorted by meaning in a number of ways. The phrases should be written on cards in their entirety, allowing students to read the phrases as a single unit. Here are a number of phrases taken from the first half of *The Memory Coat* (Woodruff 1999).

in a small town	little wooden houses	large and lively families
in the midst of this and that	fly out the door	the best of friends
in the alley	behind the synagogue	at these times
outdoors in the cold	spent many a frosty afternoon	

These phrases can be sorted in a number of ways and can be worked with before and after reading the selection. The more ways in which the phrases are grouped, the more opportunity students have to read each phrase.

2. Go over the phrases. Have students read the phrases orally, discuss what they mean, and use them in sentences.

3. Have the students work with the phrases on their own, grouping the various phrases into categories: those containing the word *in*, those containing four words, those containing the word *the*, any justifiable category.

4. Specify categories into which the phrases should be grouped. For example:

> Phrases that explain where something is
> Phrases that describe something
> Phrases that refer to time
> Phrases that remind them of something or someplace in their life
> Phrases that remind them of something or someplace in a friend's life
> Phrases that remind them of something or someplace they have read about
> Phrases that remind them of something or someplace they would like to be

5. Have students share their grouped phrases and their connections.

6. Have the students use these phrases to predict what will happen in the story.

■ Connecting It to Independent Reading

The text used to select vocabulary for word and phrase sorts should be available for independent reading. Explain to students that as they read silently they should try to read complete words and phrases.

■ Bringing It Home

Have students take the words and phrases home and read them to family members. Ask them to look for similar words and phrases in the books they read at home.

■ Using It with English Language Learners

Word sorts allow English language learners to analyze pieces of the word and become familiar with common letter patterns. Phrase sorts enable them to examine the meaning of small chunks of text. A more able student or a parent volunteer should work with English language learners to make sure their pronunciation is correct.

■ What to Read

Word sorts and phrase sorts can be set up using words from almost any book. Pick words that can be grouped into a couple of different categories. Poems written in meaningful phrases can also be used with this strategy.

Primary Titles

Bracelet (Uchida 1996)

Horace and Morris But Mostly Dolores (Howe 1999)

The Very Busy Spider (Carle 2003)

Intermediate Titles

Aunt Flossie's Hats (and Crab Cakes Later) (Howard 1991)

Freckle Juice (Blume 1971)

Nettie's Trip South (Turner 1987)

Chunking Words

24

■ What Is It, Why Use It?

This strategy is a way for students to approach unknown words in meaningful text. When consistently employed, it will increase the number of rapidly recognized words, thereby speeding up reading rate and improving comprehension.

Fluent readers do not sound out words letter by letter but look for "chunks" or recognizable parts of a word. One way students may divide a word into chunks is by letter sounds and patterns, focusing on onsets and rimes (Fox 2000). An *onset* is the beginning sound of a word that comes before the vowel, like the *sh* in *shark* or the *b* in *bark*. A *rime* is the vowel and consonants that end the word—for example, the *ark* in *shark* and *bark*. Affixes are another kind of word chunk. A word chunk may also be a smaller word within a larger word. Teachers often tell students to find the two small words that make up a compound word.

As children begin to hear and see patterns or parts within words, they use this knowledge to decode new words (Hiebert & Raphael 1998). For example, suppose your students encounter the sentence, "It was unfortunate that Jeremy lost his ten-dollar bill," and trip over the word *unfortunate*. You might begin by asking whether they see any small words or "almost words" they can recognize or pronounce. They may mention the words *fort* and *nate*. Then you could ask if they can see any prefixes or suffixes in the word, and they might come up with *un*. They have now recognized three sounds, un/fort/nate. By relying on other cuing systems, such as semantics and syntax, students may now be able to recognize the word. Analogies and rhymes can also help students pronounce and remember words. For instance with a word like *pantry,* you could suggest that it sounds like the two words *pan* and *tree.*

A "sight word" is one that is immediately recognized as a whole and does not require word analysis for identification (Harris & Hodges 1995). Sight words are also defined as words that students do not need to decode (Cecil 2003). They do not chunk parts of the word but instantly recognize the whole word, taking in the word as a chunk. Students become more fluent as they increase the number of words they can immediately recognize and understand. Eventually students are also able to chunk meaningful phrases when they read.

■ Using It in the Classroom

Word chunking helps students recognize more words more quickly. If you cover part of a word, such as the *a* in *ahead,* have the students read *head,* and then tell them to add the *a* sound, you're instinctively using this strategy. If you teach it directly, students will be able to apply it independently. Remember, though, that instruction should always take place surrounded by context, in which semantics can also be brought to bear. Direct instruction of word chunking should be abandoned once the children have internalized this strategy as part of their independent reading.

Word Chunking in a Nutshell

1. Select a number of words students have had difficulty reading.

2. Show these words in context on the overhead or on a large piece of chart paper. For example, take the following sentences from the chapter "The Day of Judgment," in *A Long Way from Chicago* (Peck 1998):
   "I don't think Grandma is a very good *influence* on us." (p. 61)
   "The *depression* is upon us." (p. 63)
   "Mary Alice stared up at her, *transfixed.*" (p. 66)

3. Begin with the word *influence.*
   - Hold up the word on a card or write it on the board.
   - Ask students if they see any little words in the big word.
   - After they have said *in* and *flu,* cover all but the *ence* and ask how this might be pronounced.
   - Have students put the three sounds together to read *influence.*
   - Read the word in context and discuss the meaning.

4. Repeat the process with the remaining words.

Variations and Applications

- *Chunk search.* After students have completed their assigned reading, have them look back over the text for words with common word patterns to use for chunks. For instance, they may find words like *singing, praising, laughing* (with the *ing* chunk) or *nation, sensation, elation* (with the *tion* chunk). In the latter case you would need to discuss the *sh* sound of the *ti* in *tion.*

- *Mystery word* (Cunningham 2000). Give the students two, three, or four multisyllabic words. Explain they are to use one chunk of each word to make a new word. Also give them a sentence that contains semantic and syntactical cues. For example:

    Using one chunk each from the words *portable, playing,* and *transfer,* make a word that completes this sentence: The truck was _____ vegetables from Florida to New York.
    Answer: The mystery word is *transporting.*

    Here's an easier example:

    Using one chunk each from the words *someone* and *anything,* make a word that completes this sentence: "Has _____ seen my math book?"
    Answer: The mystery word is *anyone.*

- *Connect-a-chunk.* Take several words in a story or textbook your students are reading, choose several affixes, and put them together with the original words to form new words. For example, you might chose the action words *jump, run, walk,* and *play* and the affixes *ing, re,* and *ed.* Possible ways to connect the chunks include *jumping, playing, walking, jumped, played, walked, replay, rerun.*

■ Connecting It to Independent Reading

Students need to be encouraged to use the word-chunking strategy independently. Here's an appropriate motto for the primary grades: "One, two, three, then ask me." This means that during independent reading students are to do three things before asking you what a word is:

1. Look at the word parts; divide it into chunks if possible.
2. Read the sentence again, followed by the next sentence or two, to see if they can find a hint about what the word might be.
3. Quietly ask a friend.

Intermediate students might use the SSCD strategy (Devine 1989): look at the *Structure* (including chunks), look at the *Sentence*, look at the *Context*, and finally look the word up in the *Dictionary*.

▨ Bringing It Home

Some parents may not be familiar with word chunking. You can send home a connect-a-chunk sheet (Appendix I) and encourage students and families to play this game together. The words brought in to us on this sheet have been as few as eight and as many as twenty. (Our respondents have created a total of twenty-seven different words—perhaps you can find more!)

▨ Using It with English Language Learners

The chunking strategy helps English language learners pronounce words by letting them do so in sections; learning a word in a foreign language is easier if a native speaker says the word slowly, enunciating each sound. (Of course, the word must then also be articulated as a single, smooth entity.)

Word chunking can also help English language learners understand affixes, but this aspect can be more confusing (Freeman & Freeman 2000). For instance, the word *replay* means play again, but the *re* in *relax* does not have the do-again meaning. You'll need to make these changing meanings clear to your English language learners.

▨ What to Read

Look for books that have words with similar chunks. Picture books are especially helpful in teaching the chunking strategy, because the pictures clue readers in to the meaning of the words. For instance, in the book *The Perfect Pet* (Palatini 2003) the words *dripping soapy water* are part of a sentence opposite an illustration in which Mom's hair is dripping down the page. Books that contain a number of words with the same affix reinforce the pattern of that particular chunk.

Primary Titles

Mouse Paint (Walsh Stoll 1992)

Rocks in His Head (Hurst Otis 2001)

The Squiggle (Schaefer 1996)

Intermediate Titles

Abiyoyo (Seeger 1996)

Ebony Sea (Smalls 1995)

The Perfect Pet (Palatini 2003)

25

Chunking Phrases

■ What Is It, Why Use It?

When asked how she can read so fast, fifth-grader Emily replies, "I just scan my eyes along the line without even thinking of reading. I automatically read." Emily has already learned the strategy of picking up meaningful phrases in one glance as she moves her eyes across the page. The ability to scan words meaningfully, in all its complexity, becomes second nature to most readers. Others need guidance, encouragement, and strategies in order to read with more fluency and understanding. In Emily's words, "Some reading skills just take lots of time to develop."

Once students have gone beyond decoding to chunking words and are able to recognize a number of words on sight, they need to be encouraged to absorb more text at a single glance. Chunking phrases helps train readers to take in a number of related words each time their eyes stop and to read this chunk of words automatically, with accuracy and expression, picking up context and meaning. With practice they are able to view more words at a time, increasing their eye span and decreasing the number of times their eyes stop per line (Weaver 2002).

For instance, fluent readers automatically chunk the sentence *the huge boy ran down the street and through the woods* into syntactically appropriate units (Rasinski 2003): *the huge boy / ran down the street / and through the woods.* Each phrase in the sentence denotes meaning, brings an image to the reader, but the whole is needed for full comprehension. Fluent readers are able to chunk meaningful phrases—and to rechunk the words differently if meaning is not attained (Weaver 2002; Rasinski 2003).

The reading of phrases, like the reading of sentences, relies on expression and prosodic cues. Reading phrases aloud using correct intonation and pauses brings meaning to the forefront. On the other hand, students need to be aware that in nonfiction some phrases (like *for example* and *for instance*) caution the reader to slow down and pay attention (Harvey & Goudvis 2000).

■ Using It in the Classroom

You can teach phrase chunking explicitly during a minilesson in which you show students how to break up a sentence into meaningful units. (Disfluent readers will benefit more if you work with them in a small group.) Students need to be able to recognize most words in the text on sight in order to chunk larger sections of text without becoming overwhelmed or frustrated.

Phrase Chunking in a Nutshell

1. Choose an interesting bit of text to share with the class. This can be a descriptive passage, a humorous poem, or a piece of exposition that contains easily identified meaningful phrases.

2. Project a transparency of this material or rewrite it on chart paper so that everyone can see the words.

3. Model correct intonation, expression, and pauses as you read the selection aloud to your students.

4. Call their attention to and model the meaningful phrases you chunk together as you read. Explain that grouping words together accomplishes two things: (1) you read them faster because you see them almost as one word, and (2) you understand the words as a unit.

5. Ask the students some of the following questions to get them thinking about the strategy:
   - How do I make the phrases sound different?
   - What meaning do you get from this phrase?
   - Could I chunk this differently by using more or fewer words?

6. Introduce different text and have your students chunk the sentences into phrases.

7. Discuss how they went about it. Ask:
   - Where did you chunk?
   - Can you read this chunk orally with expression?
   - What meaning does this phrase have?
   - If you don't understand this chunk of words, how might you chunk the sentence differently?
   - Can you add more words to the chunk and still grasp the meaning?

8. Have the students, in collaborative groups, chunk additional material into phrases. Observe to be sure they are doing it correctly.

Variations and Applications

- *Partner phrasing.* Give students text they can mark up. Ask them to read the material with a partner and discuss how they would chunk the sentences. If each partner has a different opinion, they will need to discuss their respective reasoning and arrive at a consensus. Have them mark the chunks they agree on by putting a line between the words that separate meaningful units. Walk around and assess the results. If their phrases don't convey the meaning of the sentence, tell them that sometimes they'll need to rechunk the material so that it makes more sense and flows more naturally. Help them by making suggestions if necessary.

- *Phrase pirates.* Ask students to become reading "pirates." Have them "steal" three or four interesting phrases from their independent reading. Then have them take two of their partner's phrases and use them in a sentence. Share the phrases as a class, and encourage students to use these interesting phrases in their own writing.

- *Particular phrases.* During independent reading encourage students to search for a particular type of phrase to share with the class or post on a phrase wall. To reinforce grammar, you could ask older students to identify and collect noun, verb, or prepositional phrases. First model and discuss the kind of phrase you want them to identify. Or have them collect two or three phrases that do not make much sense out of context, then share the phrases and explain what they mean in the context they found them. (The following confusing phrases from *Joey Pigza Loses Control* [Gantos 2000] make much more sense in context: "follow the prescription" [p. 18]; "with a grin rocking back and forth" [p. 20]; and "slicked all the way forward" [p. 21].)

- *Poetry phrases.* Discuss poetry phrases in terms of their purpose in the poem. First read the poem to the students. Have the class reread it orally with you.

Then allow students to pick out favorite phrases to read. Discuss the purpose of the phrase: does it create an image? evoke a feeling? tell a fact? convey humor?

▦ Connecting It to Independent Reading

Keep the materials you use for direct instruction on chunking strategies available for independent reading. Repetitive-pattern books are helpful because they contain one or two phrases that can be taught in a chunk and then practiced during independent reading. Have student partners discuss where a sentence can be separated into meaningful chunks and then practice reading the material aloud with the proper expression and intonation. Monitoring how these phrases are being separated and read ensures that your students are learning proper phrasing and expression and will be able to understand and enjoy their independent reading.

▦ Bringing It Home

Encourage family members to read to their children. Modeled reading has been shown to improve reading speed, accuracy, phrasing, and expression (Worthy & Broaddus 2002). Chunking phrases can be practiced at home. After students are familiar with "partner phrases," have them do this activity with family members. Suggest that caregivers occasionally activate the closed-caption feature of their television sets.

▦ Using It with English Language Learners

Preview text with English language learners before asking them to try chunking it. If students have problems chunking phrases, make a copy of the text and "mark up" the meaningful phrases. Then have students practice reading these phrases with the correct expression and pronunciation. Make sure English language learners have a partner who is English proficient.

▦ What to Read

Select books that are somewhat "literary." For highly disfluent students, pattern books with phrases that repeat work well. Make sure typography doesn't interfere. Some "cute" books whose print wiggles, circles, or slants appeal to the eye but are not well suited to practicing the reading of phrases.

Primary Titles

Hondo & Fabian (McCarty 2002)

Just Me and My Puppy (Mayer 1985), or any other Mercer Mayer book

Seasons (Gould 1986)

Intermediate Titles

In the Piney Woods (Schotter 2003)

My Rotten Redheaded Older Brother (Palocco 1994)

The Wall (Bunting 1990)

Paired-Reading Log

Name: _____

DAY	DATE	PARTNER	TEXT READ	MINUTES READ	COMMENTS
Monday					
Tuesday					
Wednesday					
Thursday					
Friday					
Saturday					
Sunday					

Paired-Reading Response

Partners' Names: _____ & _____

Date: _____ Text Read: _____

Minutes Read: _____

Comments: _____

_____

_____

_____

_____

_____

_____

_____

_____

_____

_____

How was _____ (reader)'s . . .

- Reading rate _____
- Expression _____
- Phrasing/chunking _____
- Accuracy _____

4	3	2	1
Great	Good job	OK	Needs Improvement

←—————————————————————→

Dear Parents and Caregivers,

When you help your child read at home, we suggest you use "paired reading," a technique that has proven very successful in improving children's reading. Paired reading is an easy, comfortable way for you and your children to share books while giving them lots of valuable practice. The steps for paired reading are below. You can use any kind of reading materials—books, magazines, and newspapers. The important thing is to choose material your child loves at the appropriate reading level.

Text for paired reading should never be too hard, but a few challenges are okay. To get you started, I've written a few suggestions at an appropriate level for your child below. Please be in touch if you need other ideas:

- _____
- _____
- _____
- _____

The steps for paired reading are:

1. Let your child select reading material at the appropriate level. You may suggest texts, but your child should be allowed to choose texts that interest her or him.

2. Find a comfortable reading spot.

3. Before reading, establish silent signals that your child can use to indicate when she or he wants to read solo and when she or he is tired and needs a break. In the latter case, you take over, reading for a short time until your child once again joins you.

4. Begin reading in unison.

5. If your child makes a mistake, then corrects the word, praise her or him. When your child makes an uncorrected mistake, wait five seconds, and then tell the word. After your child says the correct word, continue reading in unison until she or he gives you the signal that she or he wants to read alone.

6. After the reading, you and your child should talk about "how it went." Praise your child's efforts and indicate areas where she or he can improve.

7. You might also discuss difficult words or interesting ideas in the text, centering your child's thoughts on meaning.

8. After the reading, please complete the enclosed "paired reading log." This should come back to school with your child every Monday, when she or he will receive a new log.

Although I suggest your child read daily at home for at least 15 minutes, please try to have at least three paired reading sessions each week. Thank you for your help and support with this exciting, supportive way to read with your child. Please be in touch if you have questions.

Dear Parents and Caregivers,

I am writing to suggest you try shared reading with your child—a fun, comfortable way to read that helps build all skills and strategies. In shared reading, children follow along in the text while observing an expert—you in this case—reading with smoothness and expression. Sometimes you might ask your child to read along with you or reread a part of the text. Also, when words and phrases are repeated or easily predictable, you might pause and ask your child to supply them.

Shared reading is best done in texts that are just a little too difficult for your child to read alone—not too hard and not too easy. As you and your child explore and share books and other print materials, he or she will gain valuable experience in all kinds of literature without having to worry about "performing" for you.

I suggest that you make time for shared reading as often as possible, in addition to asking your child to read every night for at least 15 minutes. Some ideas for shared reading material are:

- Different versions of familiar stories

- Cartoons, comic strips, jokes, and riddles

- Children's magazines

- Stories that you and your child write together

- Poems

- Song books

Possibilities for shared reading are endless! You and your child should select materials together, finding what is most interesting and exciting for you. Thank you for your help in supporting your child's reading and our language arts program. Please be in touch if you have questions.

Listen to Me Read!

Name:

_____

Book:

_____

Read this book to five people and ask them to sign the paper. When you have five signatures bring the paper back to school.

. . . .

We enjoyed listening to the book:

1. Please sign

_____

2. Please sign

_____

3. Please sign

_____

4. Please sign

_____

5. Please sign

_____

Character Share Sheet

Name:_____ Date:_____

Interesting dialogue: What are the characters saying?

Interesting sentences to practice and share:

What feeling do I want to show? Why?

Readers Theatre Script:
The Three Little Pigs

Once upon a time there were three little pigs. They went out in the world to seek their fortunes.

The first little pig built a house of straw. No sooner was he inside than a big, bad wolf came along and said, "Little Pig, Little Pig, let me come in!"

The little pig said, "No, no, no, not by the hair of my chinny-chin-chin!"

So the wolf huffed and he puffed and he blew the house in and ate up the first little pig.

The second little pig built a house of sticks. No sooner was he inside than a big, bad wolf came along and said, "Little Pig, Little Pig, let me come in!"

The little pig said, "No, no, no, not by the hair of my chinny-chin-chin!"

So the wolf huffed and he puffed and he blew the house in and ate up the second little pig.

Now, the third little pig built a sturdy house of bricks. No sooner was he inside than a big, bad wolf came along and said, "Little Pig, Little Pig, let me come in!"

The little pig said, "No, no, no, not by the hair of my chinny-chin-chin!"

So the wolf huffed and he puffed and he puffed and he huffed, but he could not blow the house in.

The wolf climbed up on the roof and looked down the chimney. He said, "Little Pig, Little Pig, I'll get you yet!"

The third little pig put a boiling pot on the fire and when then wolf came down the chimney, he opened the lid, the wolf fell in and "POP!" that was the end of the big, bad wolf.

The third little pig lived happily ever after in his sturdy brick house.

Readers Theater Script:
The Pot That Would Not Stop Boiling

Once upon a time there was a girl who lived with her mother in a little house. They were very poor and did not have much to eat.

One day, the girl went into the woods to find something to eat. She met an old woman. "Why are you in the woods, my dear?" said the woman, and the girl told her.

The woman gave her a pot. She said, "This is a magic pot, my dear. When you are hungry, say, 'Cook, little pot, cook,' and you will have sweet porridge. When it is full, say, 'Stop, little pot, stop!' and it will stop."

The little girl thanked her and ran home with the pot to show her mother. When they needed food, the girl would say, "Cook, little pot, cook," and when they were full, she would say, "Stop, little pot, stop!"

One day, the girl was away from home. Her mother was hungry, so she took out the pot and said, "Cook, little pot, cook," and the pot was soon full.

Then the mother said, "No more, little pot, no more," but the pot kept boiling. The porridge spilled over the brim and onto the floor.

"Halt, little pot, halt!" she cried, but the pot kept boiling.

Soon the porridge ran out the door and down the street to the town where the girl was visiting. When she saw the porridge, she said, "Oh!" and ran home.

When the girl reached the house, she said, "Stop, little pot, stop!"

Instantly, the pot stopped boiling. By that time the town was full of porridge and it took the people a week to eat it all up.

Timed Repeated Reading Record Sheet

Name: _____

Name of Book or Passage:

_____

Circle One: Oral Reading / Silent Reading

Write date in the bottom box. Color in bar graph to the number of words per minute.

											WPM
											250
											230
											210
											190
											170
											150
											130
											110
											90
											70
											50
											30
											Date

Connect-a-Chunk

Using the following words and chunks of words, make as many other words as possible. Remember, you can start with the smallest word itself!

ed	honor	un	able	hurt	beat	ing	clean	cover	comfort

_____

_____

_____

_____

_____

_____

_____

_____

_____

_____

_____

_____

_____

_____

_____

_____

_____

_____

_____

_____

Children's Literature

AARDEMA, VERNA. 1981. *Bringing the Rain to Kapiti Plain.* New York: Dial Books for Young Readers.

ALLARD, HARRY, and JAMES MARSHALL. 1977. *Miss Nelson Is Missing.* Boston: Houghton Mifflin.

ALLEY, R. W. 1991. *Old MacDonald Had a Farm.* New York: Grossett & Dunlap.

ANDRZAE, GILES, and GUY PARKER REES. 2002. *K Is for Kissing a Cool Kangaroo.* New York: Orchard.

ARUEGO, JOSE, and ARIANE DEWEY. 1986. *Five Little Ducks.* New York: Crown.

ASHMAN, LINDA. 2003. *Rub-a-Dub Sub.* San Diego, CA: Harcourt.

AVI. 1999. *Abigail Takes the Wheel.* New York: HarperCollins.

BAYLOR, BYRD. 1974. *Everybody Needs a Rock.* New York: Simon & Schuster.

———. 1986. *I'm in Charge of Celebrations.* New York: Simon & Schuster.

BERENSTAIN, JAN, and STAN BERENSTAIN. Various dates. The Berenstain Bears Series. New York: Random House.

BIRTLE, JASMINE. 1998. *Animal Quakers: Jokes for Kids.* London: Robinsons Children's Books.

BLUME, JUDY. 1971. *Freckle Juice.* New York: Bantam, and Doubleday Dell Books for Young Readers.

———. 1972. *Tales of a Fourth Grade Nothing.* New York: Dutton.

———. 1990. *Fudge-a-Mania.* New York: Bantam, Doubleday and Dell Books for Young Readers.

BROOKS, WALTER. Various dates. The Freddy the Pig Series. New York: Alfred A. Knopf.

BROWN, MARC. 1994. *Arthur's Chicken Pox.* Boston: Little Brown.

BROWN, MARCIA. 1961. *Once a Mouse.* New York: Macmillan.

BROWN, MARGARET WISE. 1947. *Goodnight Moon.* New York: Scholastic

BROWNING, KATE. 2000. *The Mega Joke Book for Kids.* New York: Lothian.

BUNTING, EVE. 1990. *The Wall.* New York: Houghton Mifflin.

BURCHERS, SAM, MAX BURCHERS, and BRYAN BURCHERS. 1998. *Vocabulary Cartoons.* Punta Gorda, FL: New Monic.

BUTTERFIELD, MOIRA. 1998. *The Three Little Pigs Puppet Play.* London: Heinemann Library.

CANNON, JANELL. 1993. *Stellaluna.* New York: Harcourt.

CARLE, ERIC. 1969. *The Very Hungry Caterpillar.* New York: Scholastic.

———. 2002. *"Slowly, Slowly, Slowly," Said the Sloth.* New York: Philomel.

———. 2003. *The Very Busy Spider.* New York: Philomel.

CERF, BENNET. 1999. *Riddles and More Riddles.* New York: Random House.

CHRISTELOW, EILEEN. 1989. *Five Little Monkeys Jumping on the Bed.* New York: Clarion.

COLE, JOANNA. Various dates. The Magic School Bus Series. New York: Scholastic.

COONEY, BARBARA. 1994. *Only Opal: The Diary of a Young Girl.* New York: Scholastic.

COWLEY, JOY. 1987. *Spider, Spider.* Bothell, WA: Wright Group.

———. 1989. *Mrs. Wishy Washy.* Bothell, WA: Wright Group.

———. 1990a. *The Birthday Cake.* Bothell, WA: Wright Group.

———. 1990b. *A Terrible Fright.* Bothell, WA: Wright Group.

CRAIGHEAD, GEORGE JEAN. 1993. *Dear Rebecca, Winter Is Here.* New York: HarperCollins.

CREECH, SHARON. 1997. *Chasing Redbird.* New York: Scholastic.

CRONIN, DOREEN. 2000. *Click, Clack, Moo: Cows That Type.* New York: Simon & Schuster.

DAHL, MICHAEL. 2002. *The Everything Kids' Joke Book: Side-Splitting, Rib-Tickling Fun!* Holbrook, MA: Adams.

DAKOS, KALLI. 1999. *The Bug in the Teacher's Coffee and Other School Poems.* New York: HarperCollins.

DE PAOLA, TOMIE. 1973. *Charlie Needs a Cloak.* New York: Scholastic.

———. 1975. *Strega Nona.* Upper Saddle River, NJ: Prentice-Hall.

———. 1983. *The Legend of Bluebonnet.* New York: Putnam.

———. Various dates. Fairmont Avenue Series. New York: Penguin Putnam.

DiCAMILLO, KATE. 2000. *Because of Winn Dixie.* Cambridge, MA: Candlewick.

DiTERLIZZI, TONY. 2002. *The Spider and the Fly.* New York: Simon & Schuster.

DODDS, DAYLE ANN. 2002. *The Kettles Get New Clothes.* Cambridge, MA: Candlewick.

DOWNS, MIKE. 2002. *Pigs, Giggles, and Rabbit Rhymes.* Vancouver, BC: Raincoast.

DUNN, SARA. 1991. *Poetry for the Earth.* New York: Ballantine.

DUNREA, OLIVIA. 1989. *Deep Down Underground.* New York: Macmillan.

ELLIS, VERONICA FREEMAN. 1993. *Land of the Four Winds.* Orange, NJ: Just Us.

EMBERLEY, BARBARA. 1967. *Drummer Hoff.* New York: Simon & Schuster.

EMBERLEY, REBECCA. 1995. *Three Cool Kids.* Boston: Little Brown.

FITZGERALD, JOHN D. Various dates. The Great Brain Series. New York: Dial Books for Young Readers.

FLEISCHMAN, PAUL. 1986. *I Am Phoenix: Poems for Two Voices.* New York: HarperCollins.

———. 1988. *Joyful Noise: Poems for Two Voices.* New York: HarperCollins.

FOWLER, ALLAN. 1992. *The Biggest Animal Ever.* Chicago: Children's Press.

FOX, MEM. 1988. *Koala Lou.* San Diego, CA: Harcourt Brace.

———. 1985. *Wilfrid Gordon McDonald Partridge.* Brooklyn, New York: Kane/Miller.

———. 1986. *Snow White in New York.* New York: Oxford.

GANTOS, JACK. 2000. *Joey Pigza Loses Control.* New York: Scholastic.

GERKE, PAMELA. 1996. *Multicultural Plays for Children Grades K–3.* New York: Smith & Kraus.

GIFF, PATRICIA REILLY. Various dates. Kids of Polk Street School series. New York: Dell.

———. 1992. *Showtime at the Polk St. School: Plays You Can Do Yourself or in the Classroom.* New York: Random House.

———. 2002. *Pictures of Hollis Woods.* New York: Random House.

GILES, JENNY. 1997a. *Chicken Little.* Crystal Lake, IL: Rigby.

———. 1997b. *The Little Red Hen.* Crystal Lake, IL: Rigby.

———. 1998a. *Goldilocks and the Three Bears.* Crystal Lake, IL: Rigby.

———. 1998b. *Little Red Riding Hood.* Crystal Lake, IL: Rigby.

GINSBERG, MIRRA. 1972. *The Chick and the Duckling.* Boston: Houghton Mifflin.

GOODE, DIANE. 2000. *Cinderella: The Dog and Her Little Glass Slipper.* New York: Scholastic.

GOULD, HEIDI. 1986. *Seasons.* Boston: Little Brown.

GREEN, ELOISE. 1991. *Night on Neighborhood Street.* New York: Puffin.

GREENBERG, DAN. Various dates. The Zack Files Series. New York: Penguin Putnam.

GREENFIELD, ELOISE. 1978. *Honey, I Love, and Other Love Poems.* New York: HarperCollins.

———. 1988. *Nathaniel Talking.* New York: Black Butterfly.

HADDIX, MARGARET PETERSON. 2001. *The Girl with 500 Middle Names.* New York: Aladdin.

HARLEY, BILL. 1996. *Sitting Down to Eat.* Little Rock, AR: August House.

HART, LENNY. 2000. *Seals on the Bus.* New York: Scholastic.

HASTINGS, SCOTT E. 1990. *Miss Mary Mac All Dressed in Black: Tongue Twisters, Jump-Rope Rhymes, and Other Children's Lore from New England.* Little Rock, AR: August House.

HELLER, RUTH. 1981. *Chickens Aren't the Only Ones.* New York: Grossett & Dunlap.

HILL, ELIZABETH STARR. 2002. *Chang and the Bamboo Flute.* New York: Farrar Straus & Giroux.

HILLENBRAND, WILL. 2003. *Here We Go Round the Mulberry Bush.* San Diego, CA: Harcourt.

HOBERMAN, MARY ANN. 1978. *A House Is a House for Me.* New York: Viking.

———. 1997. *One of Each.* New York: Scholastic.

———. 2001. *You Read to Me, I'll Read to You: Very Short Stories to Read Together.* Boston: Little Brown.

HOOPES, LYN LITTLEFIELD. 1997. *Condor Magic.* Fairfield, CT: The Benefactory.

HOPKINS, LEE BENNETT. 1984. *Surprises.* New York: HarperCollins.

———. 1987. *More Surprises.* New York: HarperCollins.

———. 1992. *Questions: Poems of Wonder.* New York: HarperCollins.

———. 1994. *Weather: Poems for All Seasons.* New York: HarperCollins.

HOWARD, ELIZABETH FITZGERALD. 1991. *Aunt Flossie's Hats (and Crab Cakes Later).* New York: Clarion.

HOWE, JAMES. 1999. *Horace and Morris But Mostly Dolores.* New York: Aladdin.

HURST, CAROL OTIS. 2001. *Rocks in His Head.* New York: Greenwillow.

HUTCHINS, PAT. 1968. *Rosie's Walk.* New York: Puffin.

———. 1986. *The Doorbell Rang.* New York: Scholastic.

JAMES, SIMON. 1991. *Dear Mr. Blueberry.* New York: Simon & Schuster.

KATZ, ALAN. 2001. *Take Me Out of the Bathtub and Other Silly Dilly Songs.* New York: Margaret McElderry.

KEATS, E. J. 1963. *The Snowy Day.* New York: The Viking Press.

KLINE, SUZIE. 1988. *Herbie Jones and the Monster Ball.* New York: G. P. Putnam.

KOONTZ, ROBIN MICHAL. 2000. *Why a Dog? By A. Cat.* New York: Scholastic.

KREEGER, CHARLENE, and SHANNON CARTWRIGHT. 1978. *Alaska A B C Book.* Seattle, WA: Sasquatch Books.

LANDON, LUCINDA. Various dates. Meg Mackintosh Series. New York: Little Brown.

LANDSTROM, LENA. 2003. *The New Hippos.* New York: Raben & Sjogren.

LAVERDE, ARLENE. 2000. *Alaska's Three Pigs.* Seattle, WA: Sasquatch Books.

LeSIEG, THEO. 1974. *Wacky Wednesday.* New York: Random House.

LESTER, MIKE. 2000. *A Is for Salad.* New York: Putnam & Grosset.

LEWMAN, DAVID. 2000. *Joke Book.* New York: Simon & Schuster.

LISBERG, RACHEL. 2003. *This Little Light of Mine.* New York: Scholastic.

LOBEL, ARNOLD. 1969. *Small Pig.* New York: HarperCollins.

———. 1970. *Frog and Toad Are Friends.* New York: HarperCollins.

———. 1976. *Frog and Toad All Year.* New York: Scholastic.

———. 1979. *Days with Frog and Toad.* New York: HarperCollins.

———. 1980. *Fables.* New York: HarperCollins.

———. Various dates. Frog and Toad Series. New York: HarperCollins.

MacLachlan, Patricia. 1980. *Through Grandpa's Eyes.* New York: HarperCollins.

———. 1985. *Sarah, Plain and Tall.* New York: HarperCollins.

———. 2001. *Caleb's Story.* New York: Scholastic.

Mahlmann, Lewis, and David Cadwalada Jones. 1999. *Plays for Young Puppeteers.* Boston: Play.

Mahy, Margaret. 1994. *The Rattlebang Picnic.* New York: Puffin.

Martin, Ann. Various dates. The Babysitters Club Series. New York: Scholastic.

Martin, Bill. 1983. *Brown Bear, Brown Bear, What Do You See?* New York: Henry Holt.

Martin, Bill, and John Archambault. 1987. *Knots on a Counting Rope.* New York: Scholastic.

———. 1989. *Chicka Chicka Boom Boom.* New York: Simon & Schuster.

———. 2003. *Panda Bear, Panda Bear, What Do You See?* New York: Henry Holt.

Mayer, Mercer. 1985. *Just Me and My Puppy.* Racine, WI: Racine.

McCarty, Peter. 2002. *Hondo & Fabian.* New York: Scholastic.

McNaughton, Colin. 1994. *Suddenly!* London: HarperCollins.

———. 2000. *Don't Step on the Crack!* London: HarperCollins.

Mecca, Judith Truedale. 1998. *What a World: A Musical for You and Your Friends to Perform.* Middletown, WI: Pleasant Company.

Melser, June. 1990a. *Fast and Funny.* Bothell, WA: Wright Group.

———. 1990b. *Help Me!* Bothell, WA: Wright Group.

———. 1990c. *Just Like Me.* Bothell, WA: Wright Group.

———. 1990d. *Let Me In.* Bothell, WA: Wright Group.

———. 1990e. *Poor Old Rabbit: A Play.* Bothell, WA: Wright Group.

———. 1990f. *Sing to the Moon.* Bothell, WA: Wright Group.

———. 1990g. *Well, I Never.* Bothell, WA: Wright Group.

Merriam, Eve. 1984. *Jamboree: Rhymes for All Times.* New York: Dell.

Miranda, Anne. 1997. *To Market, To Market.* New York: Scholastic.

Mitchell, Margaree King. 1993. *Uncle Jed's Barbershop.* New York: Simon & Schuster.

Munsch, Robert. 1985. *Thomas' Snowsuit.* Munsch for Kids Series. New York: Annick.

Murphy, Claire Rudolf, and Jane G. Haigh. 2001. *Children of the Gold Rush.* Portland, OR: Alaska Northwest.

Naylor, Phyllis Reynolds. 1992. *Josie's Troubles.* New York: Yearling.

Nye, Naomi Shihab. 2002. *19 Varieties of Gazelle: Poems of the Middle East.* New York: Greenwillow.

OSBORNE, MARY POPE. Various dates. *The Magic Tree House Series.* New York: Random House Books for Young Readers.

———. 1995. *Afternoon on the Amazon.* New York: Random House.

OSBORNE, WILL, and MARY POPE OSBORNE. 2001. *Rain Forests: A Nonfiction Companion to Afternoon on the Amazon.* New York: Random House.

PALATINI, MARGIE. 2003. *The Perfect Pet.* New York: HarperCollins.

PALOCCO, PATRICIA. 1994. *My Rotten Redheaded Older Brother.* New York: Simon & Schuster for Young Readers.

PARISH, HERMAN. 1999. *Amelia Bedelia 4 Mayor.* New York: Scholastic.

PARKER, BETH. 1990. *Thomas Knew There Were Pirates in the Bathroom.* Windsor, Ontario, Canada: Black Moss.

PARKES, BRENDA. 1986. *Who's in the Shed?* Crystal Lake, IL: Rigby.

PARKS, BARBARA. Various dates. *The Junie B. Jones Series.* New York: Random House Books for Young Readers.

PATENT, DOROTHY HENSHAW. 1998. *Bold and Bright, Black and White Animals.* New York: Walker.

PATERSON, KATHERINE. 2002. *The Same Stuff as Stars.* New York: Clarion.

PAULSEN, GARY, ed. 2003. *Shelf Life.* New York: Simon & Schuster.

PECK, RICHARD. 1998. *A Long Way from Chicago.* New York: Scholastic.

PECK, ROBERT NEWTON. *Soup Series.* New York: Dell Publishing Group.

PRELUTSKY, JACK. 1983. *The Random House Book of Poetry for Children.* New York: Random House.

PUGLIANO, CAROL, and CAROLYN CROLL. 1999. *Easy-to-Read Folk and Fairy Tale Plays.* New York: Scholastic.

RAE, JENNIFER. 1998. *Dog Tales.* Berkeley, CA: Tricycle.

RAPPAPORT, DOREEN. 2002. *No More! Stories and Songs of Slave Resistance.* Cambridge, MA: Candlewick.

RATHMANN, PEGGY. 1995. *Officer Buckle and Gloria.* New York: Scholastic.

ROSE, DEBORAH LEE. 2000. *Into the A, B, Sea.* New York: Scholastic.

ROSEN, MICHAEL, and HELEN OXENBURY. 1989. *We're Going on a Bear Hunt.* Boston: Little Brown.

ROSEN, MICHAEL, and ARTHUR ROBINS. 1990. *Little Rabbit Foo Foo.* New York: Simon & Schuster.

ROWLING, J. K. 2003. *Harry Potter and the Order of the Phoenix.* New York: Scholastic.

RYLANT, CYNTHIA. Various dates. *Henry and Mudge Series.* New York: Aladdin Paperbacks.

SCHAEFER, CAROLE LEXA. 1996. *The Squiggle.* New York: Crown.

SCHOTTER, RONI. 2003. *In the Piney Woods.* New York: Farrar Straus & Giroux.

SCIESZKA, JON. 1989. *The True Story of the Three Little Pigs.* New York: Scholastic.

———. 1991. *The Frog Prince Revisited.* New York: Scholastic.

SEEGER, PETE. 1996. *Abiyoyo*. New York: Macmillan.

SENDAK, MAURICE. 1970. *In the Night Kitchen*. New York: HarperCollins.

———. 1987. *Chicken Soup with Rice*. New York: Scholastic.

SIMON, SEYMOUR. 1991. *Earthquakes*. New York: Mulberry.

SHANNON, DAVID. 1998. *No, David!* New York: Scholastic.

SHANNON, GEORGE. 1996. *Tomorrow's Alphabet*. New York: Greenwillow.

SHARMAT, MARJORIE WEINMAN. Various dates. The Nate the Great Series. New York: Dell Yearling.

SMALLS, IRENE. 1995. *Ebony Sea*. Stamford, CT: Longmeadow.

SMITH, ANNETTE. 1997. *The Gingerbread Man*. Crystal Lake, IL: Rigby.

SNICKET, LEMONY. Various dates. A Series of Unfortunate Events. New York: HarperCollins.

SOBOL, DONALD. Various dates. Encyclopedia Brown Series. New York: Bantam.

STEAD, TONY. 2000. *Should There Be Zoos? A Persuasive Text*. New York: Mondo.

STINE, R. L. Various dates. The Goosebumps Series. New York: Scholastic.

TABACK, SIMMS. 1999. *Joseph Had a Little Overcoat*. New York: Penguin Putnam.

TANG, GREG. 2003. *Math-terpieces: The Art of Problem Solving*. New York: Scholastic.

THOMAS, SHELLEY MOORE. 2000. *Good Night, Good Knight*. New York: Dutton Children's.

TRIVIZAS, EUGENE, and HELEN OXENBURY. 1993. *The Three Little Wolves and the Big Bad Pig*. New York: Simon & Schuster.

TROLL, RAY. 2002. *Sharkbet: A Sea of Sharks from A to Z*. Portland, OR: WestWinds.

TRUSSELL-CULLEN, ALAN. 1999a. *Cinderella*. Carlsbad, CA: Dominie.

———. 1999b. *The Miller Who Tried to Please Everyone*. Carlsbad, CA: Dominie.

———. 2002. *The Three Wishes*. Carlsbad, CA: Dominie.

TUNNELL, MICHAEL O. 1997. *Mailing May*. New York: HarperCollins.

TURNER, ANN. 1987. *Nettie's Trip South*. New York: Aladdin.

UCHIDA, YOSHIKO. 1996. *Bracelet*. New York: Puffin.

VIORST, JUDITH. 1981. *If I Were in Charge of the World and Other Worries*. New York: Macmillan.

WALSH, ELLEN STOLL. 1992. *Mouse Paint*. New York: Harcourt.

———. 1994. *Mouse Count*. New York: Harcourt.

WATTENBERG, JANE. 2000. *Henny-Penny*. New York: Scholastic.

WESTCOTT, NADINE B. 1988a. *Down by the Bay*. New York: Crown.

———. 1988b. *The Lady with the Alligator Purse*. Boston: Little Brown.

———. 1988c. *Skip to My Lou*. Boston: Little Brown.

———. 2003. *I Know an Old Lady Who Swallowed a Fly*. Boston: Little Brown.

WHEELER, LISA. 2001. *Wool Gathering: A Sheep Family Reunion*. New York: Atheneum Books for Young Readers.

WHITE, E. B. 1952. *Charlotte's Web*. New York: HarperCollins.

WICKSTROM, SYLVIE KANTOROVITZ. 1985. *Wheels on the Bus*. New York: Crown.

WILLIAMS, SUE. 2003. *Let's Go Visiting*. San Diego, CA: Harcourt.

WOOD, DON, and AUDREY WOOD. 1999. *Piggies*. Orlando, FL: Harcourt.

WOODRUFF, ELVIRA. 1999. *The Memory Coat*. New York: Scholastic.

WORTH, VALERIE. 1987. *All the Small Poems*. New York: Farrar, Straus & Giroux.

YOLEN, JANE. 1987. *Owl Moon*. New York: Philomel.

ZOLOTOW, CHARLOTTE. 1965. *Someday*. New York: HarperCollins.

———. 2002. *Seasons: A Book of Poems*. New York: HarperCollins.

References

ALLINGTON, R. 1983. "Fluency: The Neglected Goal. *The Reading Teacher* 36: 556–61.

———. 2001. *What Really Matters for Struggling Readers: Designing Research-Based Programs.* New York: Longman.

ALLINGTON, R., and A. MCGILL-FRANZEN. 2003. "The Impact of Summer Setback on the Reading Achievement Gap." *Phi Delta Kappan* 85 (1) (September): 68–75.

ANDERSON, R. C., P. T. WILSON, and L. G. FIELDING. 1988. "Growth in Reading and How Children Spend Their Time Outside of School." *Reading Research Quarterly* 23: 285–303.

BEAR, D. R., M. INVERNIZZI, S. TEMPLETON, and R. JOHNSTON. 1996. *Words Their Way: Word Study for Phonics, Vocabulary, and Spelling Instruction.* Upper Saddle River, NJ: Prentice-Hall.

BRUNER, J., and N. RATNER. 1978. "Games, Social Exchange, and the Acquisition of Language." *Journal of Child Language* 5 (1): 391–401.

BURRILL, NANCY, and NANCY PAULSON. 1998. *Using Paired Reading to Help Your Students Become Better Readers, Grades 1–6.* Bellevue, WA: Bureau of Education & Research (BER).

CALKINS, L. M. 1986. *The Art of Teaching Writing.* Portsmouth, NH: Heinemann.

———. 2001. *The Art of Teaching Reading.* New York: Addison-Wesley-Longman.

CAMBOURNE, B. 2001. "Conditions for Literacy Learning: Why Do Some Students Fail to Learn to Read? Ockham's Razor and the Conditions of Learning." *Reading Teacher* 54 (8) (May): 784–86.

CARBO, M., R. DUNN, and K. DUNN. 1986. *Teaching Students to Read Through Their Individual Learning Styles.* Englewood Cliffs, NJ: Prentice-Hall.

CARVER, R. P. 1989. "Silent Reading Rates in Grade Equivalents." *Journal of Reading Behavior* 21: 155–66.

CAZDEN, C. 1988. *Classroom Discourse: The Language of Teaching and Learning.* Portsmouth, NH: Heinemann.

CECIL, N. L. 2003. *Striking a Balance: Best Practices for Early Literacy.* 2nd ed. Scottsdale, AZ: Holcomb Hathaway.

CLARK, C. H. 1995. "Teaching Students About Reading: A Fluency Example." *Reading Horizons* 35: 251–65.

CLAY, M. 1993. *An Observation Survey.* Portsmouth, NH: Heinemann.

COOPER, D., and N. KIGER. 2003. *Literacy: Helping Children Construct Meaning.* Boston: Houghton Mifflin.

CUMMINS, J. 2001. *Language, Power, and Pedagogy: Bilingual Children in the Crossfire.* Clevedon UK: Multilingual Matters.

CUNNINGHAM, P. M. 2000. *Phonics They Use: Words for Reading and Writing.* 3rd ed. New York: HarperCollins.

CUNNINGHAM, P. M., and D. P. HALL. 1994. *Making Words: Multilevel, Hands-On, Developmentally Appropriate Spelling and Phonics Activities.* Redding, CA: Good Apple.

DAHL, P. R., AND S. J. SAMUELS. 1974. "A Mastery-Based Experimental Program for Teaching Poor Readers High-Speed Word Recognition Skills." Minneapolis: University of Minnesota.

DEVINE, T. 1989. *Teaching Reading in the Elementary School: From Theory to Practice.* Boston: Allyn and Bacon.

DOWHOWER, S. L. 1987. "Effect of Repeated Reading on Second-Grade Transitional Readers' Fluency and Comprehension." *Reading Research Quarterly* 22: 389–406.

FINNEY, S. 2003. *Independent Reading Activities That Keep Kids Learning . . . While You Teach Small Groups.* New York: Scholastic.

FOSNOT, C., ed. 1996. *Constructivism: Theory, Perspectives, and Practice.* New York: Teacher's College Press.

FOUNTAS, I. C., and G. S. PINNELL. 1996. *Guided Reading: Good First Teaching for All Children.* Portsmouth, NH: Heinemann.

———. 1999. *Matching Books to Readers: Using Leveled Books in Guided Reading, K–3.* Portsmouth, NH: Heinemann.

———. 2001. *Guiding Readers and Writers Grades 3–6: Teaching Comprehension, Genre, and Content Literacy.* Portsmouth, NH: Heinemann.

FOX, B. 2000. *Word Identification Strategies: Phonics from a New Perspective.* 2nd ed. Columbus, OH: Merrill.

FREEMAN, D., and Y. FREEMAN. 2000. *Teaching Reading in Multilingual Classrooms.* Portsmouth, NH: Heinemann.

GILLETT, J. W., and C. TEMPLE. 2000. *Understanding Reading Problems: Assessment and Instruction.* 5th ed. New York: HarperCollins.

GRAVES, D. 1984. *A Researcher Learns to Write.* Portsmouth, NH: Heinemann.

———. 1992. *Explore Poetry.* Portsmouth, NH: Heinemann.

GRAVES, M., and S. WATTS-TAFFE. 2002. "The Place of Word Consciousness in a Research-Based Vocabulary Program." In *What Research Has to Say About Reading Instruction,* edited by A. Farstrup and S. J. Samuels, 140–65. Newark, DE: International Reading Association.

GRIFFIN, M. L. 2000. *Emergent Readers' Joint Text Construction: A Descriptive Study of Reading in Social Context.* Ph.D. diss. University of Rhode Island.

———. 2002. "Why Don't You Use Your Finger? Paired Reading in First Grade." *The Reading Teacher* 55 (8): 766–74.

HARRIS, T., and R. HODGES. 1995. *The Literacy Dictionary: The Vocabulary of Reading and Writing.* Newark, DE: International Reading Association.

HARVEY, S., and A. GOUDVIS. 2000. *Strategies That Work: Teaching Comprehension to Enhance Understanding.* York, ME: Stenhouse.

HASBRUCK, J. E., C. IHNOT, and G. ROGERS. 1999. "Read Naturally: A Strategy to Increase Oral Reading Fluency." *Reading Research and Instruction* 39: 27–37.

HASBROUCK, J. E., and G. TINDAL. 1992. "Curriculum-Based Oral Reading Fluency Norms for Students in Grades 2 Through 5." *Teaching Exceptional Children* 24: 41–44.

HEARD, G. 1995. *Writing Toward Home: Tales and Lessons to Find Your Way.* Portsmouth, NH: Heinemann.

HECKELMAN, R. G. 1996. "Using the Neurological Impress Method." *Academic Therapy Quarterly* 1: 235–239.

HERMAN, P. A. 1985. "The Effect of Repeated Readings on Reading Rate, Speech Pauses, and Word Recognition Accuracy." *Reading Research Quarterly* 20: 553–64.

HIEBERT, E., and T. RAPHAEL. 1998. *Early Literacy Instruction.* Orlando, FL: Holt, Rinehart and Winston.

HOFFMAN, J. V. 1987. "Rethinking the Role of Oral Reading in Basal Instruction." *Elementary School Journal* 87: 367–73.

HOLDAWAY, D. 1979. *The Foundations of Literacy.* Sydney, UK: Ashton-Scholastic.

HOYT, LINDA. 2000. *Snapshots: Literacy Minilessons Up Close.* Portsmouth, NH: Heinemann.

JACKSON, A. J., and G. A. DAVIS, with M. ABEEL and A. BORDONARO. 2000. *Turning Points 2000: Educating Adolescents in the Twenty-First Century.* New York: Teachers College Press.

JIMENEZ, R. 2003. "The Interaction of Language, Literacy, and Identity in the Lives of Latina/o Students." In *After Early Intervention, Then What?* edited by R. McCormick and J. Paratore, 25–38. Newark, DE: International Reading Association.

JOHNS, J. L., and R. L. BERGLUND. 2002. *Fluency: Answers, Questions, Evidence-Based Strategies.* Dubuque, IA: Kendall/Hunt Publishing.

JOHNS, J., and S. LENSKI. 1997. *Improving Reading: A Handbook of Strategies.* Dubuque, IA: Kendall/Hunt.

KEENE, E. O., and S. ZIMMERMAN. 1997. *Mosaic of Thought: Teaching Comprehension in a Reader's Workshop.* Portsmouth, NH: Heinemann.

KOSKINEN, P. A., and I. H. BLUM. 1986. "Paired Repeated Reading: A Classroom Strategy for Developing Fluent Reading." *The Reading Teacher* 40: 70–75.

LARRICK, N. 1991. *Let's Do a Poem! Introducing Poetry to Children.* New York: Delacorte.

LESLIE, L., and J. CALDWELL. 2001. *Qualitative Reading Inventory 3.* New York: Addison-Wesley-Longman.

LEWIN, L. 2003. *Paving the Way in Reading and Writing, Strategies and Activities to Support Struggling Students in Grades 6–12.* San Francisco: Jossey-Bass.

LIPSON, M., and K. WIXSON. 1991. *Assessment and Instruction of Reading Disability: An Interactive Approach.* New York: HarperCollins.

MARCHIONDA, D. 1996. "Revealing the Humor in Reading: Using Comic Strips to Teach Comprehension and Other Reading Skills." Leaflet. Portland, ME: New England Reading Association.

MARTIN, B., and P. BROGAN. 1972. *Teacher's Guide: Instant Readers.* New York: Holt, Rinehart & Winston.

MARTINEZ, M., N. ROSER, and S. STRECKER. 1999. "I Never Thought I Could Be a Star: Reader's Theatre Ticket to Fluency." *The Reading Teacher* 52: 326–34.

MCCAULEY, J., and D. MCCAULEY. 1992. "Using Choral Reading to Promote Language Learning for ESL Students." *The Reading Teacher* 39: 206–12.

MACGILLIVRAY, L. 1997. "'I've Seen You Read': Reading Strategies in a First-Grade Class." *Journal of Research in Childhood Education* 11 (2): 135–46.

MACGILLIVRAY, L., and S. HAWES. 1994. "'I Don't Know What I'm Doing—They All Start with B': First Graders Negotiate Peer Reading Interactions." *The Reading Teacher* 48 (3): 210–17.

MINAREK, ELSE HOLMELUND. Various dates. The Little Bear Series. New York: Harper & Row.

MOSS, J., and M. R. FENSTER. 2002. *From Literature to Literacy.* Newark, DE: International Reading Association.

MULDOWNEY, C. J. 1995. "The Effect of a Paired Reading Program on Reading Achievement in a First-Grade Classroom." ERIC, ED 379634.

NAGY, W. E. 1988. "Teaching Vocabulary to Improve Reading Comprehension." Urbana, IL: NCTE.

NAGY, W. E., and R. C. ANDERSON. 1984. "How Many Words Are There in Printed English?" *Reading Research Quarterly* 19: 304–30.

NATIONAL CENTER FOR EDUCATION AND THE ECONOMY. 1999. *Reading and Writing Grade by Grade: Primary Literacy Standards for Kindergarten Through Grade 3.* Pittsburgh, PA: National Center for Education and the Economy.

NATIONAL READING PANEL. 2000. *Report of the National Reading Panel: Teaching Children to Read.* Washington, DC: U.S. Department of Health and Human Services.

NES, S. L. 1997. "Less-Skilled Readers: Studying the Effects of Paired Reading on Reading Fluency, Accuracy, Comprehension, Reader Self-Perception, and Lived Experiences." Dissertation Abstracts Online, AAG9736884.

NORTON, B. 2003. "The Motivating Power of Comic Books: Insights from Archie Comic Readers" *The Reading Teacher* 57 (2): 140–47.

OHLHAUSEN, M. M., and M. JEPSEN. 1992. "Lessons from Goldilocks: 'Someone Has Been Choosing My Books But I Can Make My Own Choices Now!'" *The New Advocate* 5: 31–46.

OPITZ, M. F., and M. P. FORD. 2001. *Reaching Readers, Flexible & Innovative Strategies for Guided Reading.* Portsmouth, NH: Heinemann.

OPITZ, M. F., and T. V. RASINSKI. 1998. *Good-Bye Round Robin: Twenty-five Effective Oral Reading Strategies.* Portsmouth, NH: Heinemann.

PEARSON, P. D., and M. C. GALLAGHER. 1983. "The Instruction of Reading Comprehension." *Contemporary Psychology* 8: n.3. p. 317–44: July 1983.

PINNELL, G. S., and I. C. FOUNTAS. 2002. *Leveled Books for Readers Grades 3–6: A Companion Volume to Guiding Readers and Writers.* Portsmouth, NH: Heinemann.

PINNELL, G. S., J. J. PIKULSKI, K. K. WIXSON, J. R. CAMPBELL, P. B. GOUGH, and A. S. BEATTY. 1995. *Listening to Children Read Aloud.* Washington, DC: Office of Educational Research and Improvement, U.S. Department of Education.

PIPER, TERRY. 2001. *And Then There Were Two.* Toronto, ON: Pippin.

PORTFOLIO ASSESSMENT TOOLKIT. 1994. Cary, IL: Designer Software for Learning. (Forest Technologies, 765 Industrial Drive, Cary, IL 60013, 800–544–3356.)

POWELL, W. R. 1980. "Measuring Reading Performance Informally" *Journal of Children and Youth* 1: 23–31.

PRESCOTT-GRIFFIN, M. L. In press, 2005. *Shoulder to Shoulder: Moving Toward Independence Through Peer Partnerships.* Portsmouth, NH: Heinemann.

RASINSKI, T. V. 1989. "Fluency for Everyone: Incorporating Fluency Instruction into the Classroom." *The Reading Teacher* 42: 690–93.

———. 1999. "Exploring a Method for Estimating Independent, Instructional, and Frustration Reading Rates." *Journal of Reading Psychology* 20: 61–69.

———. 2003. *The Fluent Reader: Oral Reading Strategies for Building Word Recognition, Fluency and Comprehension.* New York: Scholastic.

REUTZEL, D. R., and P. M. HOLLINGSWORTH. 1993. "Effects of Fluency Training on Second Graders' Reading Comprehension." *Journal of Educational Research* 86: 325–31.

RHODES, L., and N. SHANKLIN. 1993. *Windows into Literacy: Assessing Learners K–8.* Portsmouth, NH: Heinemann.

RICHEK, R., A. LIST, and J. LERNER. 1983. "Reading Problems: Diagnosis and Remediation." *The Reading Teacher* 23 (4): 130–35.

SAMUELS, S. JAY. 1997. "The Method of Repeated Readings." RT Classic. *The Reading Teacher* 50 (5): 376–81.

SAMWAY, K. D., G. WHANG, and M. PIPPITT. 1995. *Buddy Reading: Cross-Age Tutoring in a Multicultural School.* Portsmouth, NH: Heinemann.

SAVAGE, J. 1994. *Teaching Reading Using Literature.* Madison, WI: Brown & Benchmark.

SAWYER, WALTER. 2000. *Growing Up with Literature.* 3rd ed. Albany, NY: Delmar.

STRICKLAND, D. S. 1998. *Teaching Phonics Today: A Primer for Educators.* Newark, DE: International Reading Association.

TIEDT, P., I. TIEDT, and S. TIEDT. 2001. *Language Arts Activities for the Classroom.* 3rd ed. Boston: Allyn and Bacon.

TOMPKINS, G. E. 2004. *50 Literacy Strategies: Step by Step.* 2nd ed. Upper Saddle River, NJ: Pearson, Merrill, Prentice Hall.

TOPPING, K. 1987. "Paired Reading: A Powerful Technique for Parent Use." *The Reading Teacher* 40: 608–14.

———. 1989. "Peer Tutoring and Paired Reading: Combining Two Powerful Techniques." *The Reading Teacher* 42: 488–94.

TOPPING, K. J., and G. A. LINDSAY. 1992. "The Structure and the Development of the Paired Reading Technique." *Journal of Research in Reading* 15 (2): 120–36.

VYGOTSKY, L. 1978. *Mind in Society: The Development of Higher Psychological Processes.* Cambridge, MA: Harvard University Press.

WEAVER, CONSTANCE. 2002. *Reading Process and Practice.* 3rd ed. Portsmouth, NH: Heinemann.

WITHERELL, N. 1998. Vocabulary Matters. Presentation given at the Annual Conference of the Massachusetts Reading Association. April 16, Sturbridge, MA.

WORTHY, J., and K. BROADDUS. 2002. "Fluency Beyond the Primary Grades: From Group Performance to Silent, Independent Reading." *The Reading Teacher* 55 (4): 334–43.

ZUTELL, J., and T. RASINSKI. 1991. "Training Teachers to Attend to Their Students' Oral Reading Fluency." *Theory into Practice* 30: 212–17.

Index

Decodable texts, 25
Decoding
    loss of reading time with, 18–19
    reading rate and, 14
Deep Down Underground, 72
Deep work, 7
De Paola, Tomi, 25
Development of Fluency Chart (K-5), 23, 24
Dialogue, choral reading of, 65
Direct instruction, loss of reading time with, 18
Dog Tales, 122
Don't Step on the Crack!, 61
Doorbell Rang, The, 131
Down by the Bay, 67, 95
Drama
    plays (*see* Plays (Drama))
    radio reading (*see* Radio reading)
Drawing, illustrating word walls, 115
Drummer Hoff, 118

Earthquakes, 25–26
Easy-to-Read and Fairy Tale Plays, 106
Ebony Sea, 155
Echo reading, 45
    with choral reading, 64
    with purposeful oral reading, 69
    with shared reading, 59
Economically disadvantaged students, reading skills and, 16
English language learners (ELL)
    choral reading with, 66
    chunking phrases with, 159
    chunking words with, 154
    collaborative reading with, 55
    environmental print with, 116
    fluency flexors with, 78
    getting into character with, 87–88
    humorous texts with, 136
    plays with, 105
    poetry with, 94
    prereading discussion of concepts and vocabulary, value of, 34
    purposeful oral reading with, 71–72
    readers theatre with, 99–100
    repeated reading with, 121
    shared reading with, 60
    sorting words with, 150
    text signals with, 125
    writing with, 131
Environmental print, 109–17
    classroom use, 110–15
    defined, 109–10
    with English language learners, 116

independent reading, connecting to, 115
    with parents, 116
    procedures, 110–15
    reading material, 116–17
    reading the room activity, 112–13
    value of, 109–10
    variations and applications, 114–15
    word of the day, 111–12
    word walls, 114, 115
    writing the room activity, 113
Evaluation. *See* Assessment
Everybody Needs a Rock, 95
Everything Kids' Joke Book: Side-Splitting, Rib-Tickling Fun!, The, 137
Expressive reading, 44
Eye fixations, 14–15

Fables, 88
"Facts About Camels," 63
Fairmont Avenue books, 25
Familes. *See* Parents
Family Circus, 133
Fast and Funny, 100
Fast reading, with shared reading, 59
Finger pointing, reading with, 28, 32
Five Little Ducks, 67, 95
Fluency
    versus accuracy, 5–6
    coaching for, 29–34
    defined, 3, 6
    developmental implications, 6–7
    Development of Fluency Chart (K-5), 23, 24
    importance of, 6
    instructional implications, 7
    meaning and, 6
    what fluency is not, 3–5
Fluency centers, 7–8
Fluency Check
    Student Version, 39, 40
    Teacher Version, 36, 37
Fluency flexors, 15, 44, 45, 75–79
    classroom use, 75
    defined, 75
    with English language learners, 78
    independent reading, connecting to, 78
    with parents, 78
    passage flexors, examples of, 77
    procedures, 75–77
    reading material (lists), 78–79
    sentence flexors, examples of, 76
    value of, 44, 45, 75
Fluency prompts, 33–34
Fluency tools, 31–33

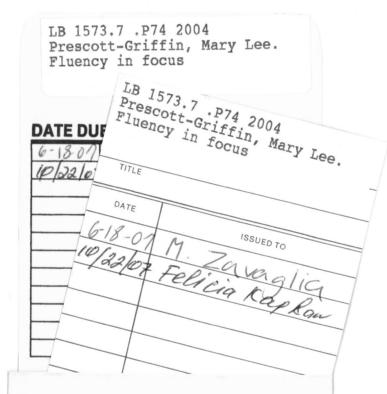